# How Grow Your Business While You Sleep

"Live the Lifestyle You Deserve
While these Breakthrough Online
Marketing Secrets Grow Your Offline
Business on Autopilot"

## By Henry Baker

George Baker Publishing

Published by George Baker Publishing,17 Chalvington Rd, Chandlers Ford, Hampshire, SO53 3DY.

This book is designed to provide information on marketing and business. it is sold with the understanding that the publisher and author are not engaged in rendering legal, accounting or other professional services. If legal or other expert assistance is required, the services of a competent professional should be sought.

Every effort has been made to make this manual as complete and as accurate as possible. However, there may be mistakes, both typographical and in content. Therefore, this text should be used only as a general guide and not as the ultimate source of marketing information. Furthermore, this book contains information on marketing that is current only up to the printing date.

The purpose of this book is to educate and entertain. The author and Publisher shall have neither liability nor responsibility to any person or entity with respect to any loss or damage caused, or alleged to have been caused, directly or indirectly, by the information contained in this book.

**If you do not wish to be bound by the above, you may return this book to the publisher for a full refund.**

ISBN: 978-0-9562835-1-1

10 9 8 7 5 6 4 3 2 1

First Edition, 2010
Published in the United Kingdom

This book is dedicated to our five month old son Henry William Baker, the love of my life Tracey and my sadly missed Dad, Steve Baker.

Thank you Tracey and baby Henry for making our ride on this rollercoaster of life so much fun.

And thank you Dad for being my inspiration – I wish you were still here.

# Table of Contents

# Acknowledgements

I must extend a huge thank you to George Baker for his invaluable suggestions after spending many, many hours reviewing this manuscript. And for his enormous assistance in the preparation of this book.

# A Magical Prescription for Change

In 1989 my late father pointed to the ceiling in our lounge and said:

"Henry... one day you'll be able to get any kind of music and any film you want at any time of day, anywhere in the world from up there."

Torn between shouting for my Mother to get the 'men in white coats', slapping him in the face, and falling on the floor in fits of laughter I slipped into my adoring son persona, looked him in the eye and said:

"Wow Dad! Really! That's awesome!"

My father was an amazing man but given I'd only just got used to MTV his statement was confusing and more than a little far-fetched.

And the more he tried to explain what he meant, the more my mind retreated into what I knew and the more weird his idea became.

How could we possibly get a film in our home

delivered without wires? Everything electronic comes down a wire, bar the radio, and that's going out of fashion.

How could there be a store of millions of music albums just 'out there' that we could listen to whenever we fancied? We listen to music on records and if we're really lucky we might get a CD player.

Well... Sorry Dad – you were right – if only I'd listened.

But even back then, deep inside me his idea had triggered something. He had stirred my creative mind and got me thinking about 'what may be'.

Fast forward about fifteen years and I'm sat in my mother's basement trying to scrabble myself out of a 'hole' having recently been made redundant for the second time in short succession.

My 'illustrious' career to that point had involved various fundamentally doomed jobs as a salesman.

Having spent a year or so completing what's regarded as the best sales training in the world with IBM; I helped them sell millions of dollars of 'kit' to small businesses. And then helped small businesses utilise e-Business in the very early days (that was IBM's term for electronic business i.e. something to do with the internet).

I built and maintained an e-Business training resource for other IBMers and then had a series of jobs with other IT (information technology) companies selling anything from smart cards to network devices to IT support services.

YAWWWWNNNNN!

Yep, you probably found the last few paragraphs about as boring as I found those years doing what I just described.

Mind numbing.

And it's no wonder that despite the high pay, benefits and perceived prestige I walked out on two of those jobs and ended up being made redundant from two more.

In hindsight maybe it did have something to do with my apparent complete lack of sales ability. I'm simply not what companies want in a salesman. The idea of 'schmoozing' clients, talking fast and closing, closing, closing makes my heart drop, my stomach churn and a feeling of complete despondency fall upon me.

I only wish my old sales manager could have heard my internal monologue and seen my smile when he told me 'I'd never be a salesman'. It went something like this.

"Thank the lord for that. If being a salesman is

ending up a hardnosed, bitter, rude, money grabbling, uneducated boring robot like you then I'd rather eat my own shoes".

Not for me thank you – I think I'll do something a little more rewarding...

The sad yet wonderfully freeing truth is I'm just completely 'unemployable'.

The endless drudgery of working for 'a company' spending all day everyday as just another insignificant cog in a machine with no soul. Playing political mind games with the 'regime' just.... isn't for me.

And I guess not for you either. As you're reading this book – I hope you are the owner or at least major player in a 'small' business.

If you own a 'big' (dumb – sorry!) business or are responsible for marketing in a 'big' business then, welcome - perhaps my simple insights will 'knock some sense' into you and save you, maybe even make you a lot of money.

But let's head back to the basement.

Sat there in my pyjamas with a mug of coffee, a biscuit and little more than a dream I decided to teach other business owners what I knew about internet marketing.

I quickly wrote a home study course on the 'basics'

(much of which hasn't changed and you'll learn in this book).

To begin, without two pennies to rub together I had to resort to manual labour. YES, I was teaching people how to utilise the internet for business but was using the telephone to find them! GASP – what a hypocrite!

But within just a few months I had turned that little business from nothing to as much as £17,000.00 a month ON AUTOPILOT, with no employees, all driven via the internet and without me having to do anything but answer a few emails and pop a few things in the post.

The business grew 24x7 and even while I slept. I'd wake up to new clients and money pretty much every day.

Ah!

It worked!

How the heck did an apparently useless at sales, corporate drop out manage that little magic trick? Well I can tell you it wasn't that hard. And I'm convinced any business owner with an ounce of common sense can put my simple system to work in their business and do much better than I did – once they understand it.

**There's nothing special about me**

I hate wearing a suit (and it'll cost you a lot to get me to wear one), love a game of tennis, enjoy a cold glass of lager as much as the next man (or lady) and get bored rather quickly. And having made my little autopilot system work, I got bored (that happens a lot), wound it down and went looking for new challenges.

I'd never planned to write this book. The only reason I'm doing so is to fend off the piles of people that 'bug' me to help them.

Having been both right in the depths of the back room, secret underground internet marketing fraternity (where most of the major online marketing breakthroughs happen by the way) and right slap in the middle of what's considered the most prestigious and highly trained sales organisation in the world at IBM (in the large part a completely misguided accolade) I have a rather unique perspective on what works and what doesn't.

And believe me I've had way more than my fair share of ups and downs, complete failures, products and services I wish I'd never created and strategies that if I'd known their outcome would never have tried. Even with the best intentions sometimes trying new things can sneak up and 'bite you on the bum'.

Pretty much everything you think you know about what works online is wrong. Most books about internet marketing are full of 'pie in the sky' theory and money sucking branding nonsense. What you see big companies doing is, with dead certainty, not right for you. Your peers and competitors are the blind leading the blind.

### This book represents an almost magical prescription for change

**_IF_** you get it, you'll beat yourself for months for not spotting it sooner without me. You'll be knocked sideways at how simple it is and how much sense it makes.

You'll see the 'wood for the trees' and never again be unsure about how you can use the internet to grow your business. You'll make major changes in your advertising and marketing, online and offline – fast.

And when you do, you'll upset some people, be criticised, argued with and maybe even laughed at. But you'll get such dramatically better results you will have the courage to ignore them and keep a little wry smile to yourself. Being thought of as different, unusual and odd, but having a bulging bank account and aggressively loyal customers is more than a fair trade.

But before we go any further please do one thing for me. Take any pre-conceptions you, your peers and colleagues have about what works, what doesn't and what might work in your industry, place it all in a cardboard box, fold the flaps to close the box, tape it shut, dig a big hole in your garden and bury it for the period of time it takes you to read this book in its entirety.

We need a clean canvas.

Growing your business while you sleep requires new skills, new strategies, an open mind and a willingness to change.

Are you ready for that challenge?

---

## **ONE NIGHT STAND?**

I've never had a one night stand and I don't intend to start now. I'd like to get to know you better and reveal some advanced strategies so powerful I left them out of this book for fear of scaring you away.

DON'T WAIT. Right now, go to:

**www.GrowYourBusinessWhileYouSleep.com/freegifts**

And follow the instructions to claim your £295.00 value of FREE BONUS resources including reports, website templates, email course that expands on this book and more.

---

## Section I

# The Foundations of Business While You Sleep

"Time is more valuable than money. You can get more money, but you cannot get more time."

- Jim Rohn

*Chapter One*

# The Costly Truth and the Big Opportunity

Most marketing, online and offline by businesses both large and small, is dreadful.

Huge quantities of money are flushed down the toilet, and life changing opportunities missed.

Most business owners are stumbling around completely unaware of the difference between a "good" website and a "bad" website, a "good" email and a "bad" email, online strategies that work and those that simply cannot.

Let alone how to setup and automate their sales and marketing process to save time, money and grow their business 24x7.

### The Myth

There's a myth that it's easy to make big money using Internet marketing with almost no risk. Nothing could be further from the truth.

I'll be completely honest with you: the worst losses I've ever taken have been on Internet marketing projects. And the worst losses I've ever seen my clients suffer were on the same.

This probably comes as no big surprise to you. Because if you have paid a lot of money for a website or to advertise online with something like Google Adwords, you know *(by the hole in your bank account)* that what I've just said is true.

Here's something crucial you should know:

***The reason you've been getting such horrible results is directly connected to the way you've been strategizing and carrying out your Internet marketing projects.***

You see, the Internet marketing techniques the average business is using today flat out do not work.

They're still based on ineffective strategies from the late nineteen nineties that didn't really work then and fail miserably now.

Times have changed radically and customer's buying habits drastically, *you simply can't afford to keep throwing money out the window* on out-dated strategies and techniques.

**Imagine you are a potential customer of yours looking to spend money on what you do...**

Where would you go to do your research? Where would you find the telephone number for your local take away, where would you go to order flowers, where would you go for pet supplies, where would you go to find someone to whiten your teeth, do your accounts, sell your house etc, etc.

The Yellow Pages?

The local newspaper?

Directory enquiries?

Flyers through your door?

The TV?

Or.... THE INTERNET????

THIS IS FACT: A recent research study found more than 25% of people have cut back on watching TV... *so they can spend more time on the internet...*

On top of that, 18% of people in the study said they were reading Newspapers less... and looking for services, getting their information, booking appointments and buying stuff on the Internet instead.

Do you buy more things on the internet - but more importantly, do you do more research about businesses you may buy from than you did 5 years ago?

What about your clients? Do you think they might just go looking for what you do on the internet?

Of course...

And keep in mind the offline stuff *(stuff not on the internet)* like the Yellow Pages, newspapers, flyers, etc you've used in the past is working less well than before, and getting much more expensive. And that trend will only continue.

## So Think About This

The good news is that all those people on the internet (a lot of whom didn't used to be) are searching for what you do on Google, Yahoo, Bing, talking with friends on Facebook and chatting away like love birds on Twitter.

That means they are literally ASKING you to be there advising them on what and why they should spend money with you. And they are easier to reach than ever before...

Take the Yellow pages for example.

All those people that used to haul out that monolithic 3kg chunk of pressed tree are now jumping on their laptops, flicking through their iPhones and heading to Yell.com or Google – typing in something they are looking for like "Dentist in Bournemouth", "Southampton Gyms", "Best plumbers in Birmingham" etc, etc and getting what they were looking for in the blink of an eye.

That's really cool news for you - really cool.

Why?

Well…

Because if it's you that jumps up first in Yell or on Google or wherever then they can be looking at YOUR ads, YOUR website, YOUR business, what YOUR clients have to say about YOU, what products and services YOU offer and buying 'stuff'; from YOU!

Without you having to lift one little finger from your lap and even while you sleep.

And you can get right in front of them in as little as 15 minutes with what I'll tell you later. Perhaps you know that already… but think about this.

### Buyers of Your 'Stuff' are Hopping Online in Droves

And you can quietly position your business right in front of these very people and essentially say:

> *"Hey, here's the info you want about the 'thing' you are looking for. And…You can even have this little gift just for dropping by (could be a voucher, a guide to what they are looking for, a consultation or whatever fits your business. As long as it's irresistible…) in return for your email address."*

To these potential customers, this is like having a friend show up, put their arm around their shoulder and say…

*"Oh. I see you're after the top provider of XYZ. Well I've got the secret place you're after and here's a bunch of their customers talking about how great the service was."*

What's great is there are more and more opportunities to do this cropping up every single day (and what's even better is that your competitors probably have absolutely no idea of the opportunity available, let alone how to tap into it).

## So...Would You Like to Know How Your Business Can _Really_ Benefit from the Internet NOW and in the Long Term?

Here's a good rule of thumb: If your products or services are high quality and can be bought by consumers or businesses, you can probably do very well on the Internet.

Some "experts" say that to be successful with the Internet, you need a product that serves a global marketplace. HOWEVER, that is simply not the case. And in fact around 60% of internet searches are for LOCAL products and services. And even better, attracting local customers is easier and cheaper that it has ever been in history.

## So, if you are a local business (and want to remain local), the Internet is fast becoming the ultimate tool for growing your business

Is the average local business or any business for that matter succeeding on the Internet today?

No, the average business is just that and the sad truth is that most businesses trying to make money from the Internet are failing miserably – simply because they don't know the success strategies that work.

What's changed is that the Internet is no longer an OPTION – it is now a necessity for any business looking for growth and it'll soon be critical.

The truth is, most of the people who are making money and successfully growing their businesses on the Internet aren't revealing their secrets.

But they're not secrets to me. And by the end of this book... They won't be for you either...

## Chapter Two

# YOUR MOST VALUABLE ASSET

Before I reveal how most brick and mortar businesses (and too many online businesses too) are throwing away an outrageously valuable asset every day I want to cover an important piece of language.

Up to this point we've referred to people who spend money with you as customers.

The dictionary defines a customer as "a person who purchases goods and services from another".

Not untrue, but not ideal either.

Even worse, in informal language you might even use the term a "tough customer" which is defined in the dictionary as "a person one has to deal with".

And quite frankly, if you're thinking that way about the people who come into your business you're going to have a hard time building a truly exceptional one.

So let's make an important language change which can only help you make a vital mind-set shift too.

From this point forward we will use the term client: "one that depends upon the protection of another" to describe our 'uh-hum' customers.

And that means if you aren't already doing so, I'd like you to start thinking of your clients as highly valued human beings who deserve and belong to be "under your protection".

### So, What is Your Most Valuable Asset?

Your premises?

Your staff?

Your product and services?

I suggest not.

Rather, the most valuable asset you can have in any business is a list of prospects and clients who trust you and are willing to buy from you repeatedly and recommend you to their friends and associates.

But most traditional brick and mortar businesses, through no real deliberate fault of their own, ignore this asset.

### Do This Exercise

For the next week, every time you visit or call a business make a note of whether or not they make any attempt to capture your name, email address, phone number, 'fax' number (I know, I know... not very popular but you'd be surprised how many people use them) and postal address.

In fact, count how many do – that way you'll have more than enough fingers to keep track!

I guarantee that only a tiny percentage of those you come into contact with will make a concerted effort to capture your details. And even less will actually follow up with you.

Out of those that DO capture your details also make a mental note of how successful they are.

Once again I'll make a guarantee. Those who DO capture your details and DO follow up with you will be markedly more successful than those that don't (and their owners a whole lot richer and less stressed out...).

### Here's What's Critical

It costs a lot of money in advertising and expenditure to get a prospect or client to walk through the front door of your business, to call you on the telephone, to send you an email or to spend money.

You MUST capture the details of as many of these people as you possible can and follow up with them.

If you don't, two critical things happen:

1. The value of the leads you generate will be much

lower.

2. The amount of money you can spend to acquire a new client will be much lower.

### So Why Do So Few 'Bricks and Mortar' Businesses Do This?

Well, how the majority of businesses in any category market themselves is largely based on how others in their category do the same.

So if most of your competitors don't do something – it's highly likely you won't either.

And in the past it has not been really cost effective for some businesses to capture leads in a database.

For example, a sandwich shop probably isn't going to make a good profit hiring telemarketers to call up their prospect and client list offering a great deal on ham 'cobs' (although if your staff were standing idle that might be worth a try!)

But if that same sandwich shop captured the email addresses and/or mobile telephone numbers of all their clients it could send a special deal offer with a voucher clients can print out on their computer or show staff on their phone any time they want.

All they have to do is send an email (or text message) which is as close to free as you can get.
They could literally generate 'cash on demand'!

BUT, for this to occur for you, you must be collecting client and prospect details. And not just haphazardly, you must have a system in place to do it on a CONSISTENT basis... And that my friend... is where we shall begin...

## Chapter Three

# MASSIVE DEMAND

We're all bombarded with thousands upon thousands of advertising messages every day. Recent research suggest somewhere in the region of 15,000 messages a day.

That's a lot – and the bad news.

The good news is that over 95% of them are about as good at stirring up emotions and getting us to go buy something as I am at knitting (dreadful).

But what is the point of all the advertising messages we see?

Well, simply to generate demand for the products and services of the companies doing the advertising.

And creating demand is the first step in our marketing system. In fact, we're going to create MASSIVE DEMAND or what I cheekily refer to as "MADNESS".

'Madness' is of course a merging or the two words 'Massive' and 'Demand' but it goes further than that.

Most businesses place far too little emphasis on

really creating a 'buzz' and excitement about what they do in the marketplace. Instead, we should aim to create real 'Madness' for what we do i.e. a massive and almost unstoppable demand for your products and services.

And how do we do that?

Well, we use every possible demand generation opportunity we can, that turns a profit, in an amount of time you decide is appropriate.

That might mean using direct mail, newspaper ads, the Yellow Pages, the radio, the TV, the Internet and endless more.

"Hold on Henry! I thought this book was about online marketing!" I hear you cry.

It is – but realise this. The true benefits of online marketing will ONLY be seen when combined with offline marketing in a coherent system designed to attract ideal clients to you, get them spending money, referring people and spending more money with you over a long period of time.

Online marketing in isolation can be very effective, but when coupled with other media the combined result is multiple times the sum of the parts.

### And this Will Really Shake Things Up

Jump onto your laptop, PC, iPhone or mobile right

now, head to Google and search for what you do in your area.

Now click on the top fifteen results.

I'm not there with you and have no way of validating what I'm about to say without sitting down with you but I'll make you a bet.

I bet that out of those top 15 maybe one, if we're lucky 3 out of those 15 websites makes any attempt at all to collect the details of the person visiting the site.

### MISTAKE COLOSSUS!

Why?

Because on average it takes 7 to 14 touches (i.e. contacts) by any particular company before we buy something.

That means that anyone not deliberately making a concerted effort to capture the details of anyone interested in what they offer is making their lives multiple times harder than need be and slashing massive chunks out of their potential profits.

Why don't they collect interested prospects details?

More often than not because they either don't realise they should or they've trusted a web designer who, while may be good at producing a pretty, graphic filled site (or sometimes not even that)... is very, very unlikely to have any experience at all in what actually makes money. Rather, they know how to give you what you think you need and how to charge you a lot for it...

If you've ever dealt with a web designer or agency – you know that's true. If you don't believe me, go find one to work with and tell them you'll pay them on results only... I doubt you'll have much luck!

Right, enough of that. Back to our plan.

### Time to Introduce You to A
### New Way of Thinking

A big round of applause and welcome please for my secret friend the "Client Magnet".

What is a client magnet?

A client magnet 'does what it says on the tin' and in almost all cases is something we give away for FREE.

Its purpose is to grab the attention of our ideal prospect (ideal client), stimulate them to sit up and pay attention to us – AND then take a specific action we ask them to take in order we COLLECT their details and can follow up with them!

Now, that action could be anything from visiting one of our websites to calling us directly, walking into our shop, coming to a seminar or any other specific action we want them to take, as long as it involves us collecting their details.

**Please take a moment to read the last three paragraphs again. Simply by making this change – you can revolutionise your business.**

For most business owners, using client magnets is a QUANTUM SHIFT in thinking.

Their purpose is NOT to sell anything (or at least very rarely) – rather, their purpose is to cut through the advertising 'clutter' that surrounds us and prompt ideal prospects to raise their hands and say "YES! Tell me more about how you can help me"...

So what constitutes a client magnet?

All sorts of different things can work very well as client magnets.

For example:

- Special reports e.g. an accountant could offer a report called 'The Insiders Guide to Choosing the Right Accountant for You". This guide would of course have the natural conclusion that the ideal accountant is the one who provided the report....

- Discounts, free gifts, coupons, free trials, free consultations...

- Videos – either offered online or on a DVD.

- Audios – again, either offered online or on a CD.

- Seminars.

- And tons more...

Exactly what you use is of course dependant on the type of client you are trying to attract, and how much you can spend to acquire that client.

A well written informative report could be a great client magnet for an affluent client of a service business, such an accountant or dentist.

A free gift could be a great client magnet for a retail store such as a jewellers or clothes shop.

A free gift voucher could be a great client magnet for a restaurant.

A free consultation could be an ideal gift for a personal trainer.

### Are You Thinking This?

If you are anything like the thousands of people I've revealed this to - then right now you'll probably be thinking something like:

"That sounds great Henry. I've no doubt my prospects would like something valuable, useful, and informative for free – but what do I get out of this deal?????"

And THAT is the question you should be asking right now.

And the answer is well... Simple...

In return for your client magnet your ideal prospects will simply leave you their contact details and give you permission to follow up with them both online and offline.

They give you permission to sell to them over and over and over again – on autopilot and almost for free.

### Have You Spotted the 'Genius' Behind this Plan?

Let's talk a little about the internet.

For most businesses their website is 'another entity'. Something they have little to do with. Something they hope people will find, like and buy from. Or...at least, something compelling enough to prompt people to call or visit their premises (although that rarely happens).

BUT, for us it is rather more than that. <u>It is the HUB, the core, the glue in our client attraction process</u>. And WHY would we want that?

Let me give you an example.

The typical business ad in the Yellow pages or a newspaper displays the company name, says what they do, usually has a telephone number and maybe a website address.

It will very, very rarely make any effort to elicit any kind of response from the person reading the ad.

But not for us...

Our ad will make a very compelling offer for our client magnet – something our ideal prospect would like (note the ideal prospect bit... you CHOOSE who you want to respond to your offer by what you give away).

For example if you are an accountant advertising in the local newspaper – no longer would we have a 'boring', 'bland', 'feeble' ad displaying your name and a list of things you do. INSTEAD, you will offer something of real value.

So, you may offer a FREE report called "101 Legal Loopholes to Reduce Your Business Tax Bill".

And to get the report prospects must head to your website. When they arrive at your website your offer is restated and in order to receive the client magnet report the visitor must leave their details. On leaving their details the report is emailed (could be posted) to them with a thank you message and instructions on what to do next.

**AND THEN YOU ARE IN A**

## WINNING POSITION

In one fell swoop you have switched yourself from being just another 'sales pest' to instead a 'welcome guest' who provides valuable information without pressure. And given that you've published a written report you're 'obviously' an authority of stature in what you do - a step above your competition.

Even better, you now have permission to sell to your ideal prospect over and over and over again.

And this has one heck of an impact on your return on advertising investment.

Why?

Well, all those people that see you newspaper ads, flyers, letters, web advertising etc, etc, would under normal circumstances, either want what you've got right then and there (a tiny percentage) or... forget all about you and when the time was right to spend money on what you do go right back to the start of their 'research'... and you'll be just another of the competing providers.

BUT NOW, because we have given them something of value and collected their details, when the time is right for them to buy, YOU, yes YOU have absolutely no excuse whatsoever for not being at the top of their consciousness.

And on top that you have PROVED yourself as an authority in what you offer and instilled the *power of reciprocity.* We humans are fickle beings and when someone gives us something, all things being equal... We will feel compelled to give in return...

If you take NOTHING else away from this book other than to collect the contact details of every prospect and client you have and then follow up with them (by email at least) with useful information and irresistible offers, then my job will be done and you can grow your business while you sleep... End of lecture...

### But Our Job Isn't Done

No, our job isn't done – far from it.

Now you have the details of someone interested in what you do; an ideal prospect – someone you have specifically chosen by the very client magnet you gave away, it's time to look after, nurture, care for that person and improve their life by helping them buy your products and services.

And here's how we do it...

## Chapter Four

# YOUR SPENDING FRENZY

The casting of roles has begun.

Most businesses are in a position of 'weakness'. Clients feel you're 'chasing them' for their money and that makes them feel uneasy and position them in control.

But things are different for you now.

Your client magnet has begun to turn you from the 'chaser' to the 'chased'; from the 'hunter' to the 'hunted' - positioning you as a 'welcome guest' rather than an 'unwanted pest'.

And now it's time to cement and enhance that position in order to gain permission to sell and create what I lovingly refer to as a "Spending Frenzy".

I call it a "Spending Frenzy" because, in comparison to the results you'll receive from bland marketing with little or no follow-up, it'll seem just that.

So...To create our spending frenzy we need to follow-up with each and every one of our prospects and clients. And just like with collecting prospect details - most businesses (of all sizes) are failing here too.

**It is up to you to influence prospects decisions, influence their emotions and influence their actions.**

And to do that you must maintain control. And how do we maintain control?

By being very, very specific about how we will follow up with each prospect and client.

And fortunately just by doing the most mundane of follow-up (and you should do much better) – you will set yourself way, way apart from your competition.

So just how do we follow-up with them?

Won't following-up with ALL these ideal prospects be mind-bogglingly time consuming?

Won't it mean you have to employ a small army of staff to make phone calls, stuff letters and send out newsletters?

Well... Those things aren't necessarily bad (and often a good idea) but...

NOPE!

There is a much simpler, cheaper, easier and much, much less time consuming way to keep in contact with your prospects. Or at least do most of the communicating for you?

What is it?

Good 'old-fashioned' EMAIL!

If you've ever bought something from Amazon then you should have spotted how they will send you an email offering something related to your initial purchase – almost every day!

This is NO accident. They do so because it is VERY profitable.

## Are You Thinking

"But we're not Amazon... We're just a local 'off-license' selling beer, wines and spirits".

Or...

"We're not Amazon, we're just a local dentist serving local patients."

Or...

"We're not Amazon, we're just a local florist serving local clients."

STOP!

It makes no odds.

Email – when used correctly (and this is where most go wrong) is the easiest, cheapest and most effective way to communicate on a regular basis with your clients and prospects to deliver timely, informative advice and offers - things that will help them.

## BUT BE WARNED

If at any point you fall into the 'mind numbing, over the head bashing sales tactics' that so many companies do... You'll instantly lose interest from huge swarms of your normally avid reading clients and prospects.

So for your audience, your collection of clients and prospects, what you send people via email is CRITICAL.

It can be the key to a new and fully laden vault of cash or a dead end met only by blank faces with wallets and purses tightly closed. We'll talk a little more about how to use email effectively later.

But for now realise that once you have distributed your client magnets, attracted interest from your ideal prospects and then captured their details – EMAIL is the first port of call for following up and beginning to build a real 'relationship' with them.

### Good News...

Now, contrary to most small business owners' beliefs (and what marketing agencies will tell you ) the good news is even a very small business can subscribe to a first class "email-autoresponder" service and send an email to all their clients and prospects automatically. YES, automatically, without any intervention from you and yes, even while you sleep.

And it's so simple.

When you offer your client magnet you make it very clear the prospect needs to head to a specific website to collect their free goodie.

On that website are the details of your client magnet and just ONE route for your prospect to take.

Leave their details in a simple form provided by your autoresponder ---- or --- leave the site.

And you should put these capture forms on every page of your website. YES, anytime someone visits your website you should try your hardest to get their details, plop them into your email and contact list and follow up with them.

If your business is more directed to people actually coming to your premises (although I've yet to find a business that can't utilise the client magnet strategy I've just revealed) then, if you have a computer online in your business you can simply enter all the contact details you want into your autoresponder and it can follow-up with your prospects and clients using targeted email messages automatically for weeks, months and even years.

And even if you don't have a computer online on

your premises, then simply collect the details on paper and enter them into your autoresponder at home...

NOTE: DO NOT confuse this with spamming. Every one of your prospects and clients will choose to be on your email list and can get off any time simply by clicking on an "unsubscribe" link in every email you send.

### But Email Is Just
### ONE Communication Media

Of course, there are lots more ways to follow up with your clients and prospects.

These include:

- Direct mail.
- Video (online and on DVD).
- Audio (online and on CD).
- The telephone.
- Fax.
- In person.

But these depend on you having those contact details to begin with – and your autoresponder system can help you here too.

You can collect a whole range of "customized fields" entering almost any kind of information you'd like to collect including phone numbers, physical addresses, the products or services a client has bought before, the products they're interested in buying, the names of your client's spouse and children... the list is limited only by your imagination.

So you can follow up in any media you wish with little more technology than a simple autoresponder (which can cost less than £20 a month).

But which media should you use for your follow up?

In an ideal world ALL of them.

### The more varied and interesting you make your follow up with your prospects and clients the better

Some people love to receive letters. Some really enjoy watching video. Others don't enjoy either of those but really appreciate one-on-one contact via the telephone. And some like all of these and more.

Ultimately the decision on which to use falls back into the hands of mathematics. How much can you afford to spend to acquire a new client and still make the profit you desire over a set time period?

Whatever you choose to use – track the cost, and track the direct impact on your profits. THEN and only then can you make an informed decision as to which are worth using for you.

But because email is so cheap (almost free at this point – it probably won't be forever though), right now it is in almost all cases the easiest and most profitable way to keep in consistent contact with your clients and prospects in a way that INCREASES your profits AND reduces the amount of time you need to spend on the follow-up itself...

### Has this Struck You Yet?

Once you have in place the system I've just described -which is so simple there's simply no excuse for not doing it; you have at your disposal an asset of enviable value:

1.  Offer client magnets – reports, discounts, gifts, trials that by their very nature attract your ideal client. You can and often should have multiple different client magnets.

    For example, a restaurant may offer a £5 meal voucher free (and have a minimum order price of £10) to new clients and could also offer a one month free trial to their wine of the month club to their most loyal existing clients.

2.  Your ideal client visits a webpage to collect their client magnet. This page has ONE purpose only – to capture the interested prospects details in return for the client magnet.

3.  You follow-up with them by email with a thank you, their client magnet and a continuous,

largely automated, email series. The email series builds rapport and moves them along your sales process. The goal being to stimulate them to spend money with you, whether that's with you in person, online, on the telephone or however you choose.

And once you have built a relationship with your prospects you can, whenever you wish, simply send a broadcast email with a pertinent offer and 'WAMMO' they'll happily give you money.

### Imagine the implications

First off a large part of your marketing process becomes completely automated. Yes, that means you can grow your business in your sleep <u>(Mental note: Yes! Henry has now shown me how to do what he promised on the cover of this book)</u>...

And picture this:

If you were a hair salon and you'd spotted on Wednesday that Thursday afternoon looked quiet you could simply email your list with a special offer like:

*"Next 5 people to book a cut and blow dry for tomorrow afternoon will receive a free bottle of wine"*

And you'll, with almost complete certainty (dependant on the size of your subscriber list and relationship), be booked solid in an instant.

Imagine you're an auto dealership approaching your year end and you have 5 cars you need to shift to hit your goals. Come up with an offer:

*"Next 5 people to secure a top of the range BMW 7 series will receive two tickets for the Monte Carlo Grand Prix."*

And 'KABOOM' you'll stand a great chance of selling them.

Imagine you're an accountant and one of the BIG 5 has just moved into your town and threatens to 'gobble up' a bunch of your clients. You could offer a special report called:

*"Warning: 7 Ways Large Accountancy Firms Will Ruin Your Business and Still Charge You a Fortune."*

You could include a 3 year upfront payment deal that locks your clients in – and/or gets you a bunch of new clients.

Imagine you own a local delicatessen, it's approaching your silver wedding anniversary and you'd like to take your husband (or wife) on a cruise. No need to pay for it out of your savings. Instead, why not start an exclusive 'Wine of the Month Club' with a wine tasting trip to France next year, email your list with an irresistible offer and 'SHABAM' you can have your cruise paid for and setup a nice monthly recurring income too!

## BUILDING A LIST OF PROSPECTS
## CAN BE LIFE CHANGING

Never before in history has this type of instant communication at such a low cost, on such a big scale and with such little effort been possible.

YET, more than 9 out of 10 small and local business owners (and a huge chunk of big businesses too) have simply not realised just how important this is.

You can grow your business while you sleep. And your list of subscribers, when treated right, is nothing short of a gold mine that can keep you in style for the rest of your life...

## Chapter Five

# Never Ending Profits

Let me ask you a question:

If I can show you a way to have all your overheads, wages and bills paid for on the first day of the month before you've even seen one client; would you be prepared to put away all your industry norms, personal hang ups and feeling of 'but my business is different' – and just do it?

Good.

Because that's what this chapter is all about: your "Never Ending Profit Machine".

I first realised its power while doing a 5km run on a tread mill at my local gym about 8 years ago. I was on the last 1km, pushing hard and trying to keep my mind off my puffing and panting. I'd renewed my membership that day and 'plumped' for the joint membership of £64 per month (which was clearly good value as a single membership was £44 and my fiancée had wanted to join).

My membership number was 2,343 and I'd asked the chap at the gym if that was the number of members they had. His response was 'No, some of those have expired, we have around 1,700.'

### Ok...back to the treadmill...

I did some quick maths in my head. £44 times 1,700. Umm, that's £74,800 a month. Even if 50% are joint membership that's still £64,600...Per month...Every month, even before anyone has been to the gym!

But what really got my attention was whenever I'd been in the gym (and I had until recently been going twice a day), there were never more than about 15 people in there!

### I finished my run and red faced, sweating, I stumbled over to the gym manager, legs like lead, and asked him:

Of your active members, how many actually use the gym?

Did the active members that didn't use the gym complain about the money they'd paid but not used?

His answers were as I expected. Only about 20% of members used the gym, and they'd only had 2 people ask for their unused gym money back in 18 months!

That means they can sail through even the most severe of recessions. Plus their stable cash flow means they can easily allocate big 'chunks of change' to go find the best, most affluent new members and spend a lot of money to get them!

Had they been reliant on single transactions, not knowing how they were going to do from one month to the next, they would have needed to be frugal about spending money.

You can and SHOULD use this model in your business immediately. A percentage of your clients will happily pay you a certain amount of money every month, automatically billed via direct debit or credit card, in return for two things:

1. Getting more monetary value than they pay for. If they are automatically billed for £30 a month, they get £50 a month in value (example only).

2. Treat them as VIPs'... Have a range of VIP 'bragging' benefits e.g. fast booking, dedicated booking number, free gifts, member lounge, and member parking...

For a local business having just a hundred people on a program like this at just £30 a month would mean £3,000 in revenue on the first day of the month before you've seen one client. A thousand would equal £30,000 a month. Your opportunity here is of course dependent on what you do and who you serve.

And keep in mind it's not difficult to sell when you offer more value, ease of use and exclusivity to those who join your recurring program. In fact, it can be a real bargain for your members.

Here are a few examples of recurring programs to get you thinking:

- Wine of the month club.
- Book of the month club.
- Retail MONEY – this can work for ANY retail business and indeed restaurant. You bill your clients X amount of money each month and in return they receive X plus Y in vouchers (or whatever form you like) to spend with you.
- Trip of the month club.
- Newsletters.
- Audio CD of the month.
- DVD of the month.
- Sweets of the month.
- Socks of the month (yes I have actually seen this in the real world).
- Access to an online membership site with all sorts of benefits for your clients.

And the list goes on and on.

Right now you might be thinking 'Yeah, but my clients won't go for that'.

Firstly, ANYONE can say that. There's no genius in 'poo-pooing' an idea.

Secondly, your clients WILL, if the offer is presented correctly and if the value is there, not only want to join but really, really appreciate you even offering the program to them.

## Here's How to Collect Your Automatic Profits

There are quite a few options for collecting recurring payments.

You can do it manually of course. Simply ask your new members to complete an enrolment form and then run those through your credit card machine each month. Time consuming, but it works.

You can setup an internet merchant account (often with your existing credit card processor) and then use an online shopping cart system such as 1shoppingcart.com. This can make things even easier as members can enrol online and the billing happens automatically in the background.

You can use an alternative online payment system such as PayPal. While PayPal can be a bit of a pain the proverbial, the upside is that, because so many people are used to using it with eBay, they do trust it...

## How to Get Clients to Stay

As long as you provide good value to your clients, keeping them in your never ending profit machine shouldn't be an issue.

However, there are advanced tactics we can use to

maximise retention and also ascension to higher levels of monthly billing. Those are outside the scope of this book, but come and talk to me if you'd like to know more ☺.

## *Chapter Six*

# The 6-Step System

Ok, we've covered an awful lot already and having completely changed the purpose of your website it's possible I've offended both you and your web designer.

I won't apologise for that because, quite frankly, if you've been using a 'normal' brochure type website then you should be apologising to yourself for being such a 'twit'... and your web designer or whomever advised you to have it should be saying sorry to you too... with a big bag of cash as an apology.

*NEVER again will your website be a little used, glossy, brochure hanging around alone in cyberspace with almost zero, zilch, zippo chance of ever bringing you clients.*

Instead, it's going to be a critical piece of your overall marketing system. A system designed to attract and keep you the best, highest paying, highest referring clients.

So, to recap...Our marketing system is as follows:

### Step One

You create one or a number of Client Magnets.

Each client magnet is designed to attract the attention of your ideal client for a particular product or service.

If you have a number of distinct products and services you may need a number of different client magnets for maximum response.

Your client magnet should be something irresistible to your ideal client. It automatically selects and attracts that person.

It could be anything from a free report, to a gift, a prize draw, a consultation, a free trial, discount or a plethora of other things.

### Step Two

You offer your client magnets to the marketplace by advertising them in as many types of media as prove profitable in a period of time you choose..

That could be could be traditional offline methods such as newspaper ads and flyers OR, online methods such as Google Adwords, search engine optimisation etc (we'll come to these in a bit).

Rather than leading with your company name, your logo and a list of your products and or services; you are now actively offering your client magnet.

You are 'selling' your client magnet NOT your products and/or services.

This is a CRITICAL change for most small businesses (and even more so for big businesses – if only they'd listen...).

## Step Three

In order to collect their client magnet your prospect is prompted to visit a specific page on your website devoted ONLY to offering the client magnet.

The webpage can be part of your existing website or in many cases will be a standalone webpage (URL). This webpage has the single purpose of 'selling' your client magnet.

In order to receive their client magnet prospects must leave their details. AND/OR, you can also collect details of those who want their client magnet in your store, office or wherever.

## Step Four

By entering their details your prospect is placed into your email autoresponder which automatically sends their client magnet (if it can be sent electronically) and follows-up with your prospect via email.

You can set up a pre-defined sequence of emails to be delivered at certain intervals to your prospects. At this point your roles are cast – you've switched from the person selling, and 'unwanted pest' to instead – a 'welcome guest'.

**NOTE:** Email is not the only media in which you can follow up with your prospects at this point. We could send them an instant SMS text message thanking them for requesting their report, or even leave them an automated voice message (called a voice broadcast) with a personal welcome from you. Both of these will of course distinguish you from your competition in an instant – apply for a one-on-one consultation to discuss these.

### Step Five

We can now continue to communicate with your prospects by email, AND for maximum profits, lots of other media too such as letters, faxes, video, postcards, voice broadcasting, SMS etc.

The point of this is to build rapport with and educate your prospects about why you're the best choice for them, as well as position yourself as the provider of choice and expert in your field.

Part of our communication is making offers for your products and services which, because you are now a trusted advisor, a much higher percentage than normal will buy. And that means lots of lovely profits for you.

### Step Six

Next... To eradicate cash flow problems forever, free up your time and to allow you HUGE competitive advantage through the ability to spend more to get a client, you kick start your never ending profit machine by offering your recurring billing product to your clients and prospects.

A percentage of your prospects and clients will accept your offer and your never ending profit machine is running.

## That's It

So your entire philosophy has switched from just trying to sell to people when they happen to be at your website, in store or in your restaurant, to instead building LONG TERM relationships with your target market through on-going communication as part of your marketing system.

And on top of that you'll be building an extremely valuable database of clients and prospects, PLUS a rock solid recurring revenue stream which means if you ever want to sell your business it could be worth multiple times more than the average in your industry.

Twenty years ago because of the cost of the consistent communication we were using this would have been, for most small businesses, cost prohibitive. BUT, now, with email it is almost FREE!

And devastatingly profitable...

## Section II

# Transforming Your Business

*"There is nothing wrong with change, if it is in the right direction."*

*- Winston Churchill (1874 – 1965)*

*Chapter One*

# How to Create Client Magnets

First, off, please don't 'stress'; about creating your client magnets. It's really easy, good fun and, once done, incredibly satisfying, and very, very profitable.

As we've discussed, your client magnets can take all sorts of different forms from reports to discounts, freebies, trials etc, etc (and we discuss many of them as we go through this book).

In this chapter we'll cover in depth what is, without a shadow of a doubt, the best client magnet in over 80% of situations I come across. The free report...

And here's why.

Whatever business you're in from butcher, baker to candlestick maker, your prospects (and your clients) have lots of questions they'd like answered and lots of information they'd like to know.

So...What questions do your prospects and clients ask you and staff over and over again?

**A well written report can answer prospects**

## questions, free you and your staff's time and place you in a position of TRUSTED ADVISOR

And being considered a trusted advisor and 'friend' is way better than being just another provider of what you do...

So... Inside the report you provide high quality information that helps your prospect save money, make money, lose weight, feel happier, feel healthier, look smarter, smell better, run faster, jump higher, choose the right car, choose the right dentist, choose the right house, maximise the value of their house, remove tattoos, choose tattoos, stop drinking beer, drink more beer or whatever it is they want to do that your product or service helps them do.

The great thing about creating these client magnet reports is it FORCES you to think about how you can really help your prospects and clients in their lives.

And THAT is what people really want. At the base of any purchase decision is an emotion. And while there is a long list of emotions we all want to fulfil you'll do pretty well if you focus on what I consider the top four:

- Health
- Wealth
- Love
- Recognition

Your report gives you the opportunity to tell stories

about you, your family and your clients and how your products and service help people in those four emotional areas.

Doing that will set your sales soaring and create a bond with your clients and prospects like nothing you've ever seen.

And to help you here's my secret four step method that creates client magnets so effective they can get a prospect to throw money at you while you sleep (joke). The four areas to think about are:

1. Interest and desire.
2. Bonding and trust.
3. Proof.
4. Sample.

Each step is fairly self-explanatory but let's walk through each in turn.

### Interest and Desire

First off – we need to be offering something that truly creates Interest & Desire.

The 'something' you use is up to you but as you now know I recommend a 'report' which SOLVES a problem or provides a BENEFIT to your prospective (and even current) clients.

For example, if you owned a beauty salon or spa you could create a report called:

## "The Consumers Inside Guide to Surgery Free Facelifts"

The report would do a few things:

1. Talk about why people think they need facelifts and how an 'old' face can make people feel 'ugly', unattractive, vulnerable etc.

2. The reasons surgical facelifts are not always a good idea.

3. The options for surgery free facelifts and why YOU are the best place to get them...Including testimonials from the clients whose lives you've changed.

Or, we could have a report for a slightly different target audience called:

## "7 Ways to Eradicate Wrinkles"

The report would do a few things:

1. Talk about why people get wrinkles and how bad they feel with them.

2. Expose some of the myths about how to remove them.

3. Give 7 treatments they can use to eradicate them, whilst making it obvious YOU are the best person to deliver those...

In these examples we are EDUCATING our prospects about their health and beauty. And in turn we NATURALLY position ourselves as the experts in that subject AND create a natural desire in them to use us.

So, now what I want you to do is grab a pen, a piece of paper and name three topics about which you could write a quick Interest & Desire report. Or, if you like add them in here:

Topic 1:
Topic 2:
Topic 3:

Easy right?

But, I'll bet you had a little moment during that process when your brain asked, "Yeah but how am I going to write a whole report about that?"

Don't worry; it happens to me almost every time. I'm a believer in allowing your subconscious mind to solve problems for you.

And I've found that over and over again, all I have to do is write down what my problems are and a solution usually represents itself "magically" in a day or two.

So just humour me on this one and write down three "sticking points" that might trip you up when it comes to writing these reports.

Sticking Point 1:
Sticking Point 2:
Sticking Point 3:

And finally let's pretend that you just took a pill that's made you the single most intelligent and productive person in the world. Hypothetically speaking, what could you ...or the world's greatest expert...do to overcome these problems?

Solution 1:
Solution 2:
Solution 3:

I'll bet you feel better already. And remember, you don't actually have to DO these right now. This is just to get your brain working. When you wake up tomorrow I guarantee you'll feel very confident about your ability to actually create these client magnets.

Now let's move on to the second essential component of our clients magnets:

## Bonding and Trust

We all have an inbuilt geography to bond with people who are like us, people who have similar interests, similar struggles and strains. And we are also conditioned to trust and follow a person in authority.

Although an unrealistic example - I had a long discussion about this with my fiancée Tracey while watching the feature film "The Day After Tomorrow".

Post the seas rising and swamping New York, at one point during the film a group of about 200 people were sat relatively safe in a library on one of the upper floors.

With little food and water, a policeman took charge and advised everyone to follow him, leave the library and go looking for food and other shelter.

The lead in the film is a young man whose father advises the government on climate change. The father had told his son to stay where he was and wait as temperatures were to plummet to minus lord knows what and anyone outside would freeze solid.

When the policeman told everyone to follow him, the young man disagreed, explained what his father had told him but was almost completely ignored.

Nigh on everyone proceeded to follow the policeman who had no idea what was ahead. Needless to say those who followed the policeman perished and the young man didn't....

An unrealistic example I know – but it proves the point. People follow those in authority. And we can use that to our advantage – in a nice way.

When we are looking to create bonding and trust we need to demonstrate that we experience the same struggles, strains and joys as our prospects and demonstrate how we solved the challenges and increase the joys...That way we both bond with them AND position ourselves in authority as a trusted advisor...

PLUS, simply using our client magnets and producing valuable information positions you as an authority naturally.

So – here we need to construct a story which allows us to both create a bond and trust with your ideal target audience.

All you have to do for this section is write down the topic.

As an example let's continue with the assumption you own a beauty salon or spa.

You'd like your ideal clients (affluent ladies and gents) to know that you're a real person, that you love to look and feel your best and that you know what you're talking about. You'd also like to create a sense of instant empathy with them so that they say, "Hey, this guy's been where I am".

So you could simply tell the story of your first job as a beautician working for a less than 'top quality' salon.

Then you'd tell how when you started, you didn't have much experience but knew exactly how you'd like to be treated and how paying attention to detail is so important when you want to look and feel your best at all times.

And you'd talk about how the salon advised you to get things done as quickly as possible and even substitute main brand, and really good, products for cheaper ones to save costs.

Then you'd explain how that made you feel really bad and made you cross because you knew clients weren't getting the absolute best service they deserved.

And finally you'd explain how you decided to set up on your own and do things to such a high standard your treatments were good enough for the Queen.

You'd explain how you travelled all over the world to find the best new techniques, how you went to tons of seminars to learn the latest techniques and how you invested lots of your own money in making sure your employees were the best trained and happiest around. You'd wrap things up by explaining how much more important it is for you that clients leave over the moon than how much money you make.

So your answer to this section would be: The Story of Your Salon Career.

NOTE: I just made all that up of course - your story MUST be completely true.

Now it's your turn...

Right now, write down what YOU would talk about?

BONDING & TRUST STORY:

Building a bond and trust with your prospects and clients is one of the best things you will ever do. And yes, I'm sure you already do so with many, if not all, your existing clients when you and your staff are face to face with them.

The power of the client magnet report is its ability to build that bond and trust on autopilot, over and over and over again -without you or your staff raising a finger.

When used correctly they're like having an army of ultra-charismatic, trustworthy employees chatting to prospects and clients 24 by 7 on demand...

### Next - Proof!

There are all sorts of proof tools we can use.

Two of the best are testimonials from happy clients and before and after case studies.

Testimonials are simply words from your clients about how great you are. Try to make these as specific as possible. e.g. rather than just:

"Henry is great", it'd be much better to have something like:

"The treatments Henry gave me not only left me feeling 10 years younger but I ended up being chatted up by three wealthy men at a party that night. Turning them down was the most fun I've had in years!" (Again, I made that up – yours MUST be true!).

Before and after case studies are similar to the weight loss and body building ones we're all used to seeing in magazines and on the internet. Ideally with pictures, you want to provide before and after examples of your services. These can be very effective.

### The Final Piece of the Client Magnet Puzzle... Samples!

An essential piece of the puzzle is to give a sample (a giveaway).

And the reason you do this is because the sample is something so attractive it actually gets prospects (and in some cases existing clients) out of their 'over communicated', 'confused' state and into your establishment where you can set to work 'knocking their socks off' with your products and services and get them spending!

What you give as a sample or giveaway doesn't need to cost you a lot of money. And, in many cases your free report will act as a good free sample in itself. But adding an additional sample to the end of your report to get prospects to take action will always boost response... For example:

A restaurant could give away free coffee.

An accountant could give away free book keeping software (perhaps a trial...).

An estate agent could give free home information packs (although thankfully these are being phased out).

And the list goes on...

Whatever you decide to give as a sample - it MUST be VERY attractive.

Ideally you want your prospects to think "Geez, they can't be giving that away for free" and then set about proving that you do...

Brainstorm now what you could give away as a free sample....

## Bringing it all Together

To help get your mind 'ticking', here are a few example titles for free reports:

- 7 Insider Secrets To Hiring The Perfect Butler

- Top 10 Money Saving Secrets To Installing A Power Shower In Your Home

- How to get the maximum price when you sell on eBay

- 9 Fatal Mistakes That Can Kill Your Conservatory

Project

- 5 Roadblocks That Can Stop You From Passing Your Driving Test

Using numbers can make writing your report much easier. Just write down every idea you have on the topic and rearrange them in a logical order later.

And here's probably the greatest secret of all to writing your own report. I know you want to create the most valuable, high quality report you possibly can for your valuable clients and prospects.

But that mindset of trying to create exceptional quality can stand in your way. Get started now!

And write as fast as you possibly can. Just get all your ideas out as quickly as you can in one huge brain dump on paper (or on your computer screen).

Once you have something written down it is a whole lot easier to rewrite and polish. Writing fast often results in your best work because you're getting past your conscious mind and writing directly from your subconscious.

**The Most Vital Element of Your Report**

Most important of all, you want your client magnet report to guide your prospect to the next step whatever you deem that to be.

If your report offers a sample then the 'obvious' next step is for the prospect to 'use' that sample. Or, the next step may be making a purchase, booking an appointment, completing an application form or any number of other actions.

Just make sure it is absolutely clear to your prospects what you want them to do next and WHY they should do it right now...And that means you need to _create urgency_ (make a note of that – it's a BIG secret to maximum response)...

## Chapter Two

# Single Action Websites

In the last chapter we discovered how to create powerful client magnets.

We can send our client magnet reports to our prospects via email as a PDF document. And, if we wish and the 'maths' makes sense we can send a printed copy of the report in the post too. Our report will do its work and move our prospects along our sales process.

And clearly, the more prospects we collect details for, the more reports we can send and ultimately the more sales we'll make. So – how can we maximise the number of people who raise their hands and say "Yes – tell me more"?

As we discussed back in Chapter Three, when we offer our client magnets to the marketplace we ask people to take a specific action to collect that client magnet.

And while we can ask people to call us or visit us in person; both of those require manual labour which at this point – before we've 'whipped our prospects into a buying frenzy' isn't always necessary.

So, I suggest we instead ask people to visit a website to collect their client magnet.

But, that website is NOT a typical 'brochure' type website with lots of things visitors can do from look at products and services, to where you're located to pricing, and more 'stuff' like that.

Rather, it is what I refer to as a "SINGLE ACTION WEBSITE". Think of it this way.

Rather than allowing any 'Tom, Dick or Harry' to look around your home with free roam of all the rooms. Instead, imagine there is a 'guard' at the front door that screens out time wasters and shows only qualified viewers around. And even better, in the exact room order you choose for maximum impact.

A single action website acts as the 'gateway' to your client magnet.

In real terms it is a single page website with powerful benefit driven copy which offers your client magnet and gives only ONE action a prospect can take. And that action is to leave their contact details and click the button to receive your client magnet.

### Using a Single Action Website Will Send Your Number of Prospects Through the Roof!

Most small business websites make no attempt at all to collect prospects details (woops).

Even those that do will usually have a lacklustre offer like "Sign up for our newsletter" hidden away down the side or bottom of the site. These will create some subscribers. Often between 0.5% and about 5% of visitors.

However, with a single action website, conversion from visitor to prospect of 20% to 60% plus is possible and should be your target. And think about the implications.

If right now you have just 1,000 people a month visit your website and you make no attempt to collect prospect details you will of course likely create almost zero prospects (you might by fluke get 1 or 2 to call you).

If you offer a simple 'Newsletter' you may create between about 5 and 50 prospects (but do you follow up with them?).

If you use a single action website you can, with just a little testing, be collecting between around 200 and 600 prospects a month. AND you'll immediately follow up with them with an irresistible client magnet that moves them along your sales process AND a sequence of useful information and offers thereafter.

Do you think that might just lead to more clients?

Of course!

And, as you can see, it is 'brain dead' simple; just a simple switch in strategies.

### So, how do we create our single action websites?

Well, there are tons of options. You can simply add a page to your existing site that has the single action or you can create a new site with specific URL for that offer.

Either way works. A specific dedicated URL for a specific client magnet will more often than not increase response because of the perceived specialisation and lack of opportunities for prospects to go hunting for other pages on your site...

The most important element of any single action website (and any marketing piece for that matter) is the headline. This book isn't a book on copywriting so we're not going to dig any further than that.

But, to help you, on the following pages are three examples of single action websites in action right now – collecting prospects for small, local businesses.

You'll note how they all follow a similar formula (for confidentiality specific business details have been masked).

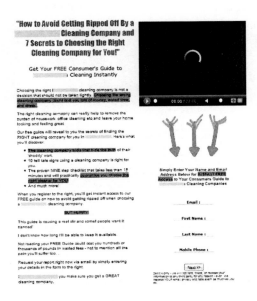

*Example Single Action Website for a Cleaning Company*

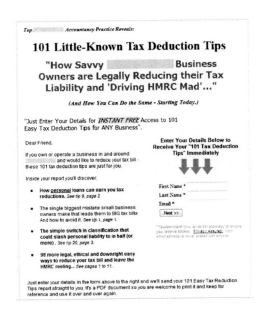

*Example Single Action Website for an Accountant*

*Example Single Action Website for a Nail Salon*

Here's another powerful benefit of single action websites. You can have as many as you like and re-use them whenever you like.

For example, every business can take advantage of seasonal events. So at Christmas you can have a Christmas specific offer and single action page. At Easter you can do the same and indeed throughout the year for different events. Tapping into seasonal events will nearly always increase response because you take advantage of a powerful marketing strategy.

## "Enter the conversation in people's minds"

Whenever you can place your marketing in tune with what the majority of your ideal prospects are thinking about at that point in time – the higher the response to your marketing will be.

And as single action websites are easy and fast to create once you get the hang of them – you can always be in tune with your prospects and way ahead of your competition.

## An Army of Automated Prospectors

Unlike sales people, single action websites work 24x7 come rain or shine, without the need for breaks, 'pep talks', company cars, sick pay and without slumps in performance.

Once you've tested and perfected the message for optimum conversion a single action website will just sit there and work tirelessly to bring you exactly the type of prospects you want.

In fact, they even keep working while you have a snooze or go on holiday for six months with the family...

## Don't Kick Yourself

When I explain single action websites to audiences for the first time their faces can't help but reveal their feeling of stupidity for not spotting these themselves. Most have for years used boring, glossy, picture laden brochure type websites and know that had they used single action websites – then right now they'd be making a lot more money than they do...

But don't worry. You're now in a very, very small 'club' of business owners who understand this simple yet devastatingly effective strategy. Just make sure you take action and start using it NOW.

---

# FREE BONUS RESOURCE

Because single action websites are so important we've created a selection of templates for you to adapt and use.

To collect your templates simply head to:

**www.GrowYourBusinessWhileYouSleep.com/freegifts**

---

## *Chapter Three*

# Prizes and Gifts

It should now be clear that rather than distinguish between online and offline marketing, we are using our website and other online media to create a marketing system which brings us ideal clients.

And it is our client magnets that begin the whole process.

For a bricks and mortar business, prizes and gifts can make excellent client magnets. And while you can get subscribers by offering almost any gift or regular prize draw, it is far more powerful to offer a highly targeted gift.

It is very wise to give away a gift that indicates anyone who takes it is almost certainly interested in a product or service you're selling.

The gift of a report: "The Small Business Guide to Choosing an Accountant" is a great example.

Only people who are looking for an accountant, or know someone who's looking for an accountant, are likely to want that report.

So you know the list you create by giving that

report away is highly targeted and filled with prospects that are looking for a small business accountant.

If you're giving away a prize, you can also keep your lists laser targeted by creating a different list for every different type of prize you give away.

### A specialist audio shop you could give away a top of the line amplifier as a prize

To enter, visitors to your store (or your website) might enter their name, email address, physical address and phone number in a coupon, in your store or in a form online.

You now have a list of people who you know are interested in that amplifier and probably general audio equipment too.

You can then follow up with them before the prize draw, telling them about all the amazing features of the amplifier...what makes it unique...why top audio experts prefer it.

Then after the draw you can send a sequence of emails to everyone who didn't win and offer them:

1. A special price if they buy by a certain date.

2. Special payment terms if they qualify so they can buy their amplifier now.

3. Notification that you only have 2 amplifiers left so time is running short if they want to claim one and you'd hate to see them miss out.

4. An offer of a lower priced amplifier that has many of the same features.

5. A super budget amplifier that has a few of the same features.

For really spectacular results simply have your staff call prospects on the telephone once or twice to make these offers.

The key here is to start by mentioning the prize draw then finding out what offer suits the prospect by asking questions.

Some will be thrilled to get a discount deal, while at the other end some will be thrilled to get a cheap amplifier anything like their dream amplifier.

What's so cool here is that by creating a unique list for the prize offer you know they're interested (or at least most of them are interested) in the type of thing the prize is and therefore you can target the offers that specific list is likely to respond to...

### And that's worth its weight in gold

You can use this exact formula to rapidly, and often dramatically, get your clients returning and spending more often in your business.

Simply make these gift offers on a regular basis by email and physically in your business with vouchers or other gift certificates.

A hair salon could have a weekly draw for a free cut and blow dry.

Clients who enter and don't win can be sent an email saying "we're sorry you didn't win the free cut and blow dry, but we really value having you as a client in our salon so here is a £10 voucher...our gift of appreciation to you."

You put conditions on the voucher to ensure you make a profit when your client cashes it in.

For example you might have conditions like: "Not valid with any other offer."

And "Limit of one voucher per client."

Most important of all you can also put a time limit on the voucher based on the average frequency your clients come to your salon.

If you know your average client visits you every 6 weeks you could give them a voucher that expires in 3 weeks' time.

That increases the "frequency" that your current clients visit you... and frequency of purchase is one of the 3 main ways to increase your sales and profits.

**The same method can be used in
Nearly any business where your clients
Buy from you repeatedly**

Give them a prize that expires...they must use it within a time period that encourages them to come in earlier and more often than they would normally.

- A gym could give out a low priced, or even free, session (and make a profit selling drink, food, equipment, clothing etc).

- A yoga teacher, naturopath or massage therapist could give a special discount price or a free ticket for a new treatment (and then book the client in for a series of follow up sessions of the same).

- A garage business could give a special price on a vehicle "check up" or oil change to help clients avoid a time wasting and costly break down (and make money selling servicing, repairs and parts).

- A cleaner could offer a special price on one room carpet cleaning, do an awesome job and then offer to do the other rooms and secure the client on a regular long term cleaning contract.

## How to Make this Work for You

Here's a simple process you can use to make this work for you:

Step 1: Focus on higher priced, high profit products and services to those who take up your discount offer.

Why?

Because if you're making a much higher profit on those back end sales you can afford to be more generous with your gift and therefore attract more people...

Step 2: Track and record how many of your clients that take up this gift or discount offer buy your back end products and services.

Step 3: Calculate your net profit from those sales and then an average per client.

That average is your average client value and THAT is the amount you can afford to spend through this method to acquire a client.

If you follow this formula, you'll see that in most cases you can afford to be EXTREMELY generous with your gift or discount because you know how much money you'll make later on.

And I can assure you, your competition will be dumbfounded as to how you can possibly give away so much... But what they'll miss is just how fast you attract new clients and just how much market share you'll snap up.

Generosity pays when offered with a plan... And as you'll see later it is one of your triggers to help your marketing message go viral.

*Chapter Four*

# Explode Your Profits and Offer Client Magnets on Every Page of Your Website

Every single page of your website should have a form where your visitors can sign up to receive a client magnet.

Use a headline above your form to tell your visitors about the valuable gift (your client magnet) they'll get when they sign up and the reasons they should look forward to opening and reading every email you send.

If you have a blog you can have your sign up form appear under every post.

For maximum response to your client magnet offer consider using a two step sign up process:

1. Have them enter their name and email address in the sign up form.

2. Have that form redirect them to a page where

you offer an extra gift which will be sent in the post (or even just sent via email) if they leave their address, telephone number, date of birth, fax number etc.

Remember the contact details of your prospects and clients are exceptionally valuable and you want to take every opportunity on your website pages to capture those details so they become part of your powerful, automated, follow up system.

## Use compelling, powerful headlines to attract prospects and clients

95% of all Websites use the company or product name or logo as the headline, or they say...

### "Welcome to XYZ"

**WRONG!** Product and company names **are not** headlines!

They don't provide any <u>benefits</u> to your visitors. This is a big mistake.

Surprisingly, it's very difficult to find Websites with compelling headlines. In fact, when I wrote an article *How to Double Your Website Response In as Little as 17 Words*, I searched the internet looking for strong Website headlines to use as examples. I went to 155 different Websites in all sorts of business categories... ***and not one had a headline I could use as an example for the article.***

When someone visits your Website, you only have a few seconds to get them engaged, so they'll stay. So it's important to use a compelling headline to make the most of that time.

A powerful headline can dramatically improve the results of a website. A headline is responsible for 90% of the success of a space ad or direct mail letter. Although I don't know of any comprehensive research on headlines on the internet, I have personally seen that using an effective headline... rather than a company name... can increase sales by over 614%.

That's incredible leverage, especially since there's virtually *no cost* to making these changes...

## You Have An Enormous Competitive Advantage If You Use Powerful, Effective Headlines!

In fact, the absence of decent headlines on the internet is shocking to me, since marketers have known for half a century how important it is to use powerful headlines (I mean just think...WHY do you pick up one newspaper over another? The headline perhaps??).

I've seen many experienced, smart marketers in other media go "brain dead" when it comes to marketing on the internet. *They seem to forget every marketing principle that has made their own business successful.* **I don't want this to happen to you!**

But you don't have to take my word for it. Here's a

simple test to see for yourself: If you currently have a Website with your company or product name as your headline (or your headline is "Welcome to the home page of XYZ"), try this...

Take what you currently have as your headline and 'bin it'. Then, develop a compelling, powerful headline that offers your client magnet (and for this test don't hang around – you should be able to conjure up a client magnet of some kind in an instant).

Ideally get your capture form and autoresponder set up on your website but if you don't have time just get them to call you directly to request their client magnet.

Use any and every available means you have to send as many potential prospects as you can to your website, starting today. Test it for a week or two. **I bet you'll be blown away by the results!**

### And Don't Be Afraid to ASK!

Every single member of your staff (and I mean every – client facing or not)  should be trained to ask everyone they come into contact with if they'd like your free gift  and follow up 'goodies' as an incentive for joining your email list.

Ask them to collect names and email addresses over the phone and when they're with clients face to face. Then simply enter them into your autoresponder and let it do its work.

Now instead of those prospects disappearing off into the wilderness to go spend money with your competitors, you can keep in constant contact with them and dramatically increase the chance they'll spend money with you.

This costs ALMOST NOTHING and can lead to real profits you would not normally see – on autopilot.

I know you won't... But don't be lazy... Put a system in place TODAY to 'capture' everyone your business comes into contact with.

## Chapter Five

# Make Your Clients Apply

If you charge an entry fee or cover charge for entry in your business you can create a special discount price for members only.

And to become a member your clients have to fill in an application form including their contact details.

The reduced or free entry fee or cover charge is the incentive for them to fill in the form but you still need to give them a compelling reason to open and read your emails.

In this case you could tell them you'll send them special member deals and offers by email and mail. If you have something really special you may even give them a call on the telephone to let them know.

Important: your prospects and clients are telling you what they're interested in when they sign up and you want to make the most of that.

You should have different lists of prospects and clients dependent on which of your client magnets they have requested.

Because remember, what client magnet someone requested tells you a LOT about what they are interested in.

If you own a shoe shop and offer two client magnets; one being a monthly 'Ladies Shoe Night' with guest designers and one being a 'Free Guide to Preventing, If Not Curing, Bunions' then of course the people on these are likely to respond to different offers. There will be some overlap BUT, you'd be wise to have different offers for each list...

In fact, by developing very specific client magnets for very specific groups of clients you can easily increase the responsiveness of those clients.

Everyone loves something that is seemingly 'just for them'.

## *Chapter Six*

# The Power of Business Cards

Now you're devising really enticing client magnets which get people literally begging to subscribe to your email list and to open and read your emails you should promote your client magnet offer in as many ways as possible.

It should appear on your business literature, brochures, flyers etc.

But most important of all you should harness the neglected power of business cards to bring you new prospects and paying clients.

On the back of your business cards you can put your client magnet offer and point people to your single action website to collect it.

For example, if you are a fitness instructor you might have on the back of your business card:

*"Free Report: The 7 Fastest Ways to a Beach Body Without Dieting, Go to www.blablablablablas.com to claim your report plus the free email series 10 Little*

*Known Secrets to Reducing Stress and Increasing Energy In Under 30 Days."*

If they give you their email address in person you can offer to enter it into your system for them. All they have to do then is confirm their email address in the confirmation email sent by your autoresponder service.

So every business card you give out becomes a powerful prospecting tool. And you can take this many steps further.

If you were running a coffee shop you could give every staff member their own set of business cards with your valuable gift offer (like a £5 coffee and cake voucher) on the back.

You could also use other incentives like a free top up or free doughnut with any drink.

Tell your staff they can give out the cards to their friends and people they meet.

Giving gifts to friends and strangers and having their own business card makes your staff feel important and it also multiplies the number of people actively promoting your business.

You have the choice of requiring your prospect to sign up to your email list to claim their free gift or you can give them the option of signing up for even more free gifts.

And you can take this even further.

For your especially loyal clients you can create a special V.I.P. card...a card they can give out to friends with a special gift offer on the back.

On the front of the card you might have something like:

*"You have been given this gift card from one of our special preferred clients."*

Now, depending on how much a new client is worth to you, it may or may not be worth going to the expense of printing your client's name on the card.

Either way, this is a powerful method for making it enjoyable for your best clients to give you high quality referrals and it can be adapted with a little thought for most businesses.

*Chapter Seven*

# How to Use Search Engines to Send You a Stampede of New Prospects and Clients

Since there are something like 60 BILLION web pages (according to Google in May 2010), perhaps the most important tools for helping people find what they are looking for are the directories and search engines. These directories and search engines provide free listings to Website owners.

Let's look at an example: your drains are blocked and you need to find a plumber in your area. So you go to one of the top search engines like Google or Yahoo (Google has a much bigger share of searches than anyone else) and you type in the keywords "plumber in Southampton" (you'd replace Southampton with your town).

You'll get back a list of all the Websites the search engine thinks are relevant for your keywords "plumber in Southampton". At the time of writing, there are 218,034 pages containing those words.

I suppose you could trawl through all those 218,034 pages, but obviously that's not practical. What you'll do is look at a few of the top sites – the sites on the first page, and perhaps the second page, to find what you want. And that's what the majority of your clients will do too...

So, the key to success is to be listed on the first page as many times as possible – if you have three mentions on the first page you'll look like more of an authority on what you do than someone with only one. And you will get a bigger share of those searching to visit your site, which will lead to more prospects and more clients.

After all, if someone is interested in your kind of product or service, you want them to find you, *not* your competitors.

And when you know how, getting to page one of Google and having multiple listings is a real possibility. That can lead to lots of traffic to your website that doesn't cost a penny (although it real terms it likely will as it takes work to get to the top of the search engines). So the question arises:

### How important are the search engines for generating website traffic?

They're very important. And the good news is that dominating them with your listings is easier than you might think.

And I bet you're wondering:

## How do I get my Web pages listed at the top of the search engines, so that people searching for my product and service find my Website?

Unfortunately there isn't a <u>"magic bullet" for success</u>, but there are some great techniques to help you succeed.

Understanding how people use search engines will also help you understand how to deliver content in a way that will serve visitors who come from search engines and turn your website into a "search engine magnet".

Let's look at an example. Say you're looking for a car. You might head to a search engine such as Google and enter "cars".

You'll quickly work out that you need to be more specific to get the results you want so you might enter "cars for sale"... what in internet language is called a "keyword phrase".

Again you'll realize you need to be even more specific so you might try "Ford Mondeo for sale".

Then you get a whole pile of results in areas where you don't want to travel to buy a Ford Mondeo.

So you might try "Ford Mondeo for sale Hampshire".

Then you might wonder if the vehicle you want is for sale in your city so you could try "Ford Mondeo for sale Southampton".

You find a whole pile of Mondeos for sale but you're looking for a used vehicle so you try "Used Mondeo for sale Southampton".

Then you think, I wonder if someone has one for sale in my town so you try "Used Ford Mondeo for sale Chandlers Ford Southampton".

We call these more complex searches "long tail keyword phrases".

There are many strategies for getting the search engines to send you traffic but one of the simplest is to target a single page on your website for each of these long tail keyword phrases.

It can be very difficult to get to the top of Google (or any other search engine) for a search term like "cars" or "cars for sale".

In fact, you'd be doing astonishingly well just to get onto the first page of result for those highly competitive search terms.

But getting to position 1 or 2 in the search engines for a long tail local keyword phrase like "Used Ford Mondeo for sale Chandlers Ford Southampton" is usually a reasonable possibility (and often very easy).

And over the course of a few months or a couple of years you can easily build 50, 100, 200, 500 or more pages on your website each targeting one of these long tail keyword phrases.

Each phrase might only bring you 1-10 visitors a day but when you add up all the visitors to each of those pages you get a whole pile of high quality, highly targeted prospects coming to your site.

Keep in mind that approximately 60% of internet searches are for 'local' things. People searching for local products, services, businesses and people. And if you are a local business that is great news.

The even better news is that because very few businesses have even the smallest amount of knowledge about how to get their websites ranked by the search engine, competition in most categories is very low and you can, with not too much effort, get multiple listings on page one of Google and the other search engines.

## The secret to multiple listings is to publish LOTS of different types of content

While you'll struggle to get two pages from your website on the first page of Google for the same keyword, you can often quite easily get a page from your website, an article, a video, a social bookmark, a blog post, a press release, a podcast and more on page one.

That means that coupled with a pay per click ad and a Google local business listing (which we'll talk about in a moment) you could have 30%, 40% even as much as 60% or more of the 'search real estate' for your best keywords.

And if a potential client goes looking for what you do, who's going to stand the best chance of earning them as a client? 'Joe Blogg's' down the road who has one listing on page one and a brochure website without a client magnet or one of your 7 listings which each contain valuable content and point visitors to your free valuable client magnet?

There'll be almost no competition for you. You'll be playing in a virtual competitive vacuum...

But for a moment, let's head back to the 'techie' stuff...

## How To Find Lucrative Long Tail Keyword Phrases

How do you find what long tail keyword phrases people are actually searching for online?

One of the most useful tools is free and from the World's largest search engine – Google.

Google's Keyword Tool will give you an idea of the search volume for a term and the number of "pay per click" advertisers competing for a search term on

Google's search engine. Right now you can find Google's keyword tool at:

https://adwords.google.com/select/KeywordToolExternal

Pay per click ads are the "Sponsored Links" you see at the top of the page and down the right hand side of the page when you do a search on Google (or on Yahoo, Bing and most other search engines).

Each time a visitor clicks on one of those ads the advertiser pays a fee.

That's why it's called "pay per click".

If there are lots of advertisers paying for ads in one search term over a long period of time that suggests the people entering that keyword phrase are spending real money online so it's probably a good phrase to target with one of your pages.

This free tool will help you get started and I know some very successful small business owners who've used nothing else but this tool.

If you want to get more advanced there are tons of services available now that allow you to literally 'spy' on what your competition is doing.

You can see what ads they're using, how much they're paying, how much traffic there is and lots more besides.

You can even track their ad campaigns to see which keyword phrases they continue to bid on over time...a good indication that those phrases are bringing them in real profits.

This is a complex, quite 'techie', area and while I and many of the most successful online marketers are self-taught – for most business owners like you, you are much better off saving your time and hiring an expert to help you.

* EDITORS NOTE: You can apply to work directly with the author Henry Baker and his team by requesting an application form at:

www.GrowYourBusinessWhileYouSleep.com/apply

## How To Make Your Page Attractive To Search Engines

Ok, now you've chosen a few keyword phrases to target, what specifically do you need on a page to attract the attention of search engines?

There are many approaches, but the quickest way to get results is to optimize your whole page for just one long tail keyword phrase.

That means:

1. You want the title in the browser window to closely match your long tail keyword phrase.

2. You want somewhere between 100 and 600 words of content in the form of text on the page tightly related to your long tail keyword phrase.

3. If you have an image on the page make sure it's also related to your chosen long tail keyword phrase and make the filename of the image similar to the phrase too.

You might have a picture of a Mondeo you have for sale and rename it:

UsedMondeoChandlersFordSouthampton.jpg, before you upload it to your website.

Using an "ALT" tag for your image similar to the long tail keyword phrase you've chosen for the page may also help your search engine rankings.

**Don't try to trick the search engines**

If you don't have an image related to your long tail keyword phrase then that's easily fixed. Just take a photo with a digital camera.

If you have audio or video on the page rename the file or title of these so they closely match your long tail keyword phrase and the content in the audio or the video.

Even though it may not affect your search engine ranking, keep in mind that your "meta description" is the description of your page most likely to appear on search engines like Google.

So make sure the description is as enticing as possible to your best prospects so they click through to your page.

## IMPORTANT: GOOGLE LOCAL BUSINESS LISTINGS

No doubt you've spotted that when you search of a local product, service or company right now in Google – the first page of results includes a map with local business listings.

What many businesses don't realise is that those listings are FREE!

Yes, Google will allow you to list your business in your local area at the top of the search engines for free...

If you haven't yet claimed your Google Local Business position do so now by visiting the Google Local Business site at:

www.google.com/local/add/businessCenter

Now, depending on how many of your competitors have claimed their listing, you may or may not be listed at the top of the page one list (or even on page one).

And being at the top if the listing or at least in the top 7 can be very lucrative... For that to happen, you need to do certain things and do them better than the other companies listing against you. For most this is a 'black art' as Google rarely, if ever, reveal their method for deciding who will rank there.

But, I've 'cracked it' and know with almost certainty what you need to do to get in the top 7 listings, if not the top position, no matter how competitive your market may be.

It's too in-depth for this book. So to help you I've created a special free guide called:

### "How to Get a Top 7 Listing on Google Maps in as Little as 24 Hours"

You can collect your free guide and other free goodies by heading to the back of this book and following the instructions... Don't miss out – loads of cool stuff. And this is very important.

### Stay Focused On Improving Your Marketing Process

Even though you should try to get maximum search engine exposure for the pages you create on your website, remember our main goal is to improve your marketing process, the sales process and the follow up process in your business.

Don't get so obsessed with search engine rankings

that you take your focus off far more powerful and profitable strategies. Search engine optimisation is a huge field worthy of an entire book of its own (and more). And it changes almost daily – which leads to a degree of uncertainty and risk. A business with a page one listing today may enjoy free visitors BUT, a slight change from Google (or any other search engine) and that page one listing could slip and those free visitors gone... Relying on one source of demand generation is NEVER a good idea – don't do it!

You can of course learn everything you need to know yourself BUT, like everything in business, you should spend your time on what you do best and let other people do the rest for you.

My team and I do work with a select few clients to provide a 'done for you' solution to everything in this book. However, that is by strict application only – partly due to the nature of our guarantee.

Details of how to apply are in the back of this book.

Keep in mind that most small businesses can massively increase their profits simply by maximizing the potential of the prospects and clients already coming into their business.

That should be where you spend most of your time - regardless of whether search engines are a major part of your demand generation strategy. The reason is simple.

By giving the best possible service to all of your clients, gaining referrals will be easier and you will make a higher profit from each client. In turn that increases the profits you make from your demand generation campaign.

And that means you can afford to invest far more money acquiring each new client. You can afford to invest more money on staff or contractors to create new web pages with content for you. You can invest more money on pay per click advertising than your competitors because you're making more money from every lead you generate.

*And that gives you a huge competitive advantage both online and offline.*

---

# FREE BONUS REPORT

If you serve a local market, having your company in the top 7 listings in Google Maps is essential. To help you I have another Free Bonus resource for you:

**"How to Get to a Top 7 Listings On Google Maps In as Little as 24 Hours"**

To collect the report simply head to:

**www.GrowYourBusinessWhileYouSleep.com/freegifts**

---

## Chapter Eight

# Blogging for Profits

If you've been online in the last 5 years or so you've almost certainly noticed the explosion of blogs.

Originally, most blogs were like online diaries filled with quite useless, self indulgent ramblings.

But in the last few years savvy marketers have started using blogs as an easy way of delivering high quality content and getting it noticed fast by search engines.

Search engines love blogs for one simple reason.

**A well designed blog is supplying constantly updating, highly targeted content**

Search engines love highly targeted content that keeps changing every time their search engine "spider" takes a look at the site.

If you have a small business and you have very little online marketing skill, putting up a blog could be the simplest way to get your business into the search engines and your unique expertise and knowledge on display.

## A 10 year old could set up a blog (and many do)

If you don't yet have a blog (or even if you do) there is only one blog provider I can hand on heart recommend. And that is Wordpress. Wordpress is in my opinion way ahead of any of the other blog platforms in usability, number of 'plug-ins' and it's search engine friendliness.

And best of all... It's FREE!

Many web hosting companies will give you one click installation of a Wordpress blog and you can also use a whole variety of Wordrpress "plugins" to add a whole range of features to your blog.

You can also choose from a range of custom designs for a Wordpress blog at:

http://themes.wordpress.net.

If you really don't fancy Wordpress then blogger.com is also quite simple to set up.

Here are a few important suggestions.

1. Get your own domain name and hosting. You can get inexpensive hosting and your own domain name from any one of a 'gazillion' providers.

2. Always give useful information that highlights the reasons your prospects should buy from you.

3. Be open with high quality useful information. Most business owners are way too worried about giving away their secrets - most of the things you think are secrets really aren't.

4. Target each post of your blog to a long tail keyword phrase, the reason being that each of your posts counts as a single web page and by targeting long tail keyword phrases your search engine visibility for those keywords will rocket.

5. Have a headline for a client magnet and sign up form on EVERY post in your blog.

   This is a huge secret to ramping up your number of email subscribers as visitors start coming from search engines to various different pages of your blog.

6. Be sure that your blog is set to "ping" automatically every time you make a post. Put simply, "pinging" your post is letting the search engines and blog indexing services know that you've just added new content to your blog.

   Both Wordpress blogs and Blogger.com blogs can be set to "ping" automatically with each post you make. This will help the search engines find your new content and index it meaning a whole lot more free visitors to your blog.

7. Enter new posts on a regular basis. At the very least once a week. Once or twice a day will usually get you the best search engine results.

If you have staff who can write useful, targeted information you can have each staff member enter a blog post once a week splitting the work between you.

In Wordpress you can enter multiple posts and have each actually appear on your blog at a time you set in the future. So you could do 7 posts for a whole week in one sitting and set them to appear one at a time each day.

You can also have multiple blogs...one for each staff member all on the same domain or on separate domains.

The more highly targeted content you are creating between you and your staff the more attention you're likely to draw from the search engines.

Also, blog posts don't have to be long to be effective at getting search engine traffic. The ideal length for a post is usually somewhere between 200 and 600 words.

But if you have a couple of images or a video in your post you could probably get away with as little as 100-250 words.

8. Use images and videos to make your blog more exciting and interesting for your visitors.
   You can create images by taking photos with an inexpensive digital camera and uploading them to your blog (most blogs have step by step instructions for this).

   You can also create a video with a digital camera or even the camera on a cell phone and upload that to a free site like YouTube or DailyMotion.com.

   Then you use the code to "embed" the video on your blog. It sounds a little complicated but it is very easy to do.

9. Part of your email follow sequence should be sending your subscribers to specific pages of your blog to read the high quality content there. This not only adds another piece of VALUE to what you do but blogs inherently help create a community as people are welcome to comment on your posts.

   And in fact you should deliberately entice people to comment. Why?

   Because comments on your blog are social proof that other people read, enjoy and respond to what you do. And social proof is a POWERFUL marketing tool.

Just like SEO, blogs are worthy of an entire book of their own. The basics I've outlined here however will set you in good stead.

The key is to keep adding keyword targeted VAULABLE content to your blog and make sure each post offers a client magnet...

But it's not just your own blog that can bring your more prospects and clients.

### How to 'Piggy-Back' Off Other People's Blogs

There's a simple way to get your site listed on the search engine results and build credibility in your industry.

Use the power of other people's forums, blogs and other interactive sites.

If you search on Google or Yahoo for keywords in your industry you'll usually find a list of blogs and forums on the topic. You should participate in blogs and forums by giving useful advice that can build your credibility in your industry.

Doing so can also give you vital links back to your website (and the more relevant links you have back to your website the higher you will appear in the search engine listings...).

Most forums allow you to create a "signature" that appears automatically under every one of your posts.

A signature is usually 2-6 lines of text promoting your own products, services or your website. And your signature can include a live link to your website.

This can be a huge advantage to you in two ways.

First, you can offer your client magnet in your signature and people who like your advice are likely to click through to your website to collect your client magnet by joining your email list.

The second advantage is the link to your site.

If the forum you post on is ranked well in the search engines that means your site is likely to get indexed very quickly and the links are also likely to improve your own search engine rankings.

When you post a comment on someone else's blog you usually get a chance to include a link to your website too and this can also lead to some valuable traffic.

## But a word of warning

If you go onto a forum or blog just trying to make some quick cash you will likely get eaten alive.

Remember these are living, breathing communities of people sharing information and guidance with each other. They don't take kindly to people entering their community just trying to 'flog' products and services.

Every forum has its own unique rules and guidelines and you must follow them or you'll most likely be banned from the forum altogether.

If you take the attitude that you're there to become part of each of these online communities and to share valuable and useful information to its members you should do well.

You can use the posts you make and the ideas you get from posting on forums and blogs as content for your own blog and website and to create information products you can give away or sell.

The best part of this kind of information is that it's a result of real questions and problems prospects in your market are having so you're laser targeting in on the solutions they're willing to pay for.

*Chapter Nine*

# How to Monetize the Largest Collection of 'Buyers' on the Planet... eBay

Google is the world's largest search engine BUT eBay is the largest collection of BUYERS on the planet.

Of over 300 million searches a day on Google many are just looking for information of various kinds and have no intention of buying anything.

At the time of writing, eBay has over 60 million searches a day and the majority of people who are searching on eBay are ready to buy.

And we'd be 'silly' not to take advantage of that.

In this chapter we'll cover my two main eBay strategies.

The first and most obvious is to simply list your product or service in an eBay auction.

Keep in mind that you can list your products at a fixed price or with a minimum bid so even though eBay is mainly an auction system it can also be used to sell products and services at a fixed price.

Selling your products and services on eBay can work especially well in categories where people are already on eBay shopping for your products.

Examples include computers, electronics, cars, antiques, jewellery, second-hand musical instruments, stamps and coins. There are many others and a search on eBay will quickly give you an idea of products you're selling now that may be worth listing on eBay.

There's even a free tool you can use that shows you the most popular searches on eBay:
http://pulse.ebay.com

One of the biggest secrets to selling effectively on eBay is to include at least one long tail keyword phrase in the title.

Remember your prospect searching on eBay still has to find your product. It also helps if your title or your subtitle gives people skimming the listings an enticing reason to click through to your eBay ad.

Then take the time to write a full, detailed description of your product in your eBay ad. You want to give your prospect all the details they need and all the reasons why they should buy this product from you.

Remember if you're selling the same product over and over again you can reuse the ad, so it's worth the extra effort of doing something really special.

And if you're selling a whole range of similar products you can copy and paste large portions of your ad to create an ad for another product.

Putting pictures of your product in your ad can also make a huge difference to your sales. If you're going to take an enthusiastic approach to listing your products and services on eBay be sure to track how much you spend on your listings and which listings produce the most views and the most sales.

You want to capitalize on methods that work and progressively dump the listings and methods that aren't working for you.

Also, eBay advertising costs are minimal, but if you're running a large number of ads the expense can add up so you want to be sure you're actually making a profit.

There's a very simple way to test out selling products on eBay. Just get some items from your own home you don't want any more and list them.

That will give you some real, live, practical experience in the whole process from listing an ad to running an auction, to taking payment and delivering the goods.

## The second strategy is a little more complex but can be many times more lucrative

You can capture your portion of the enormous traffic running through eBay by selling intentionally low priced products and then making your profits with back end sales.

Now before I go into any more detail, it's important to play fair here. If you use this strategy in an intelligent way you can make a substantial on-going income from eBay traffic.

But remember, eBay makes its money from its ad listings and creates all that traffic that you can benefit from. So don't try to cheat eBay out of its hard earned visitors...play fair and eBay will keep sending you visitors for years to come.

### Here's how the strategy works.

You focus on getting as many targeted prospects as possible to your auction listings by selling an enticing product or information report, eBook (we'll discover these in depth in a later chapter) or audio with an exceptionally low starting bid (99p).

Your objective here is exposure.

By selling a lead-in product at a low price to lots of new prospects you can quickly build your email list with real buyers.

Later, I'll reveal simple ways to create information products you can use as lead generators on eBay, as an incentive for prospects to join your email list, as a powerful way of turning prospects into high paying clients and as a source of ongoing revenue.

At the time of writing this book there's another way you can capitalize on the traffic coming to your eBay auctions.

Within the eBay terms of service you're permitted to add an "About Me" page to eBay which links to your website.

In the first paragraph of your eBay ad you can mention that they should check your About Me page for similar listings and for more free information about whatever the topic of your eBay ad covers.

Then on your About Me page you can have a link to your website where you offer your free incentive for signing up and your enticing email series.

More traffic to your eBay listings means more traffic to your About Me page and more new targeted email subscribers.

Keep in mind rules can change and you should check to see what is within the current terms of service. You don't want to break the rules and find your eBay account cancelled.

The basic strategy here is not so much about creating an "about me". What you're really doing is trying to make the most out of the traffic coming to your eBay auctions.

You could achieve similar results by selling multiple products at a very low price and following up with those buyers.

eBay also has an advertising feature as an alternative to eBay auctions that you could experiment with using this basic strategy.

One final note:

If your auction listing includes a long tail keyword phrase then that listing will almost certainly be picked up and listed near the top of the rankings on search engines like Google.

That means both your website page and your eBay listing can be at or near the top of the search engine rankings giving you multiple chances of picking up your most highly valuable targeted prospects.

## Chapter Ten

# Classified Ads are More than Just 'Lonely Hearts'

When I was younger, my brothers and I took great delight in searching through the classified personal ads in the local paper. There was something humorous to a teenager about ads that read something like:

*"Short, Receding, Tubby But Fun Man Seeks 6 Foot Long Legged Blonde Willing to Play – Models Considered."*

But of course, now I just feel for them...

Anyway, in some areas, ONLINE free classified ad sites do very well in the search engine results and can make you real sales.

In some cases, they can also give you a live link to your website.

Best of all the ads are free.

Examples of sites worth checking are gumtree.com, craigslist.com, freeads.co.uk and any other classified ad site (there are endless others all over the world) that is showing up near the top of the search engines in your town or city.

Craigslist enjoys especially good rankings in the search engines for US cities and some capital cities in other countries.

There are 2 main keys to using classified ad sites successfully.

1. For some of these sites it is against the rules to include a web link back to your client magnet distribution site. But often the same sites have no real limit on the length of your ad.

2. Use a long form ad to promote your product and services and, as with eBay, consider selling low priced products as a lead generator.

Note: Right now in craiglist.com you are allowed to include a live link back to your website (i.e. one of your single action websites). If your ad title includes a long tail keyword phrase this will often do very well in the search engines as craiglist.com is a highly ranked site.

You could shoot straight to number 1 or 2 on Google for a search term like "Bournemouth Area Landscape Gardner" for example if that is the title of your ad.

This can be a very fast way to get your website found by search engines like Google and Yahoo and get your products or services in your ad listed near the top of the search engines.

BUT, on most of these sites your ad will only run for a set period of time. That means you or your staff will need to renew the ad on a regular basis.

Keep in mind that on most sites you can have more than one ad...different ads for different products and services you offer.

Also track any results you get from these sites.

While there is a very real chance you'll make real sales or bring in real clients using online classified ads, there's also a good chance you'll be wasting your time.

Test different classified ad sites, different kinds of lead generating ads, different contact methods like straight to your website, email or phone numbers.

If you're not getting any positive results invest more time in one of the other online marketing strategies in this book where you are getting results.

Important Note: If you don't YET have a website online you can still put up an online classified ad for one of your products or services or a gift offer and use your phone number or email address as a contact method.

This is something you can be testing minutes from

now with no outlay, no website and no real online skills.

### Chapter Eleven

# The Magic of Pay Per Click Advertising

One of the fastest and most consistent ways to attract visitors to your website is with what's called pay per click advertising (PPC).

In essence, pay per click advertising means you pay a fee to another site or search engine for every visitor who clicks on an advertisement on their site and visits your site as a result.

This can be exceptionally lucrative. And, if you're advertising in a large niche the potential for rolling out a large campaign once you know your ads, and website are profitable is very exciting.

In some niches there are literally millions of people searching every day and with a PPC ad you can place yourself in front of those millions in just a few minutes.

But succeeding with pay per click advertising is a sophisticated process and most businesses are throwing their money away paying high prices for clicks and never making a penny from their visitors because their websites don't follow these key principles:

1. You must send the people that click on your ad to a webpage designed to COLLECT THEIR DETAILS in return for a client magnet.

   This page should specifically relate to the keyword they were searching for.

   Paying to send people to a brochure type of website is an utter waste of time and money and if I catch you doing it I'll have no choice but to seriously reprimand you *(in fact the amount of money you'll have wasted will be enough punishment)*.

2. You must track every visitor from pay per click advertising. You need to know:

   - What keyword they were searching for.
   - The percentage of visitors that leave their details in return for your client magnet.
   - How much money those people subsequently spend with you.

   By knowing exactly how much profit you're making from each visitor and from each ad, you can dump ads and bids on keywords that aren't making you money and continue with ads and keywords that are making you money.

   Fortunately most PPC providers include tracking options. These allow you to very tightly and easily measure your return on investment.

3. You need to bid on a large list of long tail keywords. Most pay per click advertisers make the mistake of bidding on basic keywords that are both more expensive and less likely to produce clients.

   When people search online for something they usually start with a broad search term and then get more and more specific.

   For example, if we were looking for an LED TV we might start with a search term "LED TV", get the results, look at a few sites and choose a size. We may then search for "50 inch LED TV", see the results then choose a brand and then search for the best price for that brand.

   It's not until then that we might make a buying decision.

   Now in your case you need to be there in all those keyword phrases offering your client magnet. Which in this case may be a report called "The Consumers Inside Guide to LED TVs – What the Manufacturers Don't Want You to Know".

   We'd offer the report in return for an interested prospect's contact details. We can then create a competitive vacuum and sell to them based on OUR terms – i.e. what we dictate as the things that are important when choosing an LED TV. By doing so we can avoid getting into 'price haggling' and keep your profits high.

So, it's usually far more effective to bid on lots of long tail keywords and pay only pence for clicks.

However, IF your lifetime client value is high enough – you can bid on the most competitive keywords, steal the lion's share of clicks and leave your competition dumbfounded as to how you did it *(NOTE: your never ending profit machine is the secret ingredient to exceptionally high long term client value).*

4. Split test your ads! It's not uncommon to find one ad will outperform another multiple times over. Split testing is quite easy to do. Google Adwords and other pay per click advertising providers allow you to test the "click through rates" (CTR) of two ads against each other. Click through rate is the percentage of people who clicked on your against how many times it was shown. So a CTR of 1% would mean that for every 100 times your ad was shown, one person clicked on the ad.

   You change the headline or the wording for an ad you're running and test it against the other ad.

   The ad that produces the best results becomes your "control". You continue to run the most successful ad and test another change against it over and over.

   Some people ask "when should you stop this split testing process?" The answer is never. Keep split testing constantly.

That's one of the biggest secrets to profitable pay per click advertising.

Finally, you can get a huge head start on creating a list of long tail keywords to bid on and examples of ad ideas you can adapt for your own use by looking at other advertisers in your niche online.

There are lots of pay per click "spying" programs that can scour the internet or any website you choose and give you back a list of the keyword phrases advertisers are bidding on and the ads they're using.

You can also monitor and track which ads run over a long period of time. If an ad is continuously running for 3 months or more you've got a pretty good indication that it's profitable for the advertiser.

So by taking that ad you have a good starting point.

There's no long term mileage in stealing or copying someone else's ad BUT, it's unlikely your competition will be as sophisticated as you're now becoming and you will be able to adapt what they're doing for even more success.

**BUT BEWARE**

They could (if they ever worked out how) do the same to you...One downside of some online marketing is that it is very, very visible. It's very hard to hide what you are doing at the 'coal face' - the start of your marketing funnel.

However, what you do AFTER someone has requested your client magnet is what's important. You see, making money from online marketing is rarely about big instant profits (although it can be) it's much more about building long term relationships with prospects and clients over time.

Looking for immediate sales is usually a big mistake. And a trap most businesses unwittingly fall into...

### Frankly, this is a very brief overview of pay per click advertising

Don't start a pay per click campaign without being willing to put in a lot of effort and spend some money testing. Most businesses are throwing away their money on pay per click campaigns because they simply don't understand the basics I've shown you here.

I've spent years and thousands upon thousands of pounds of my own money figuring out how to use it effectively. You're welcome to go through that process yourself but if you'd like help request an application form from the back of this book.

## Chapter Twelve

# How to Use Online Video to Multiply Your Profits

Video marketing is one of the biggest breakthroughs in marketing since the first print ad was run in a magazine.

Why?

Because it's the closest to face-to-face communication we have managed so far without actually being face-to-face.

By spending 30 minutes creating a simple webcam video, or even just a slideshow, you can produce a sales message that, when done correctly, can be more effective than any other media.

At the time of writing this book there are well over half a billion video views around the world per month. Online video is more than 60% of all online traffic and Youtube is the #4 search engine in the world.

Ignoring video is no longer an option.

But just like other types of media, using video for

profit requires specific strategies.

Recording a quick 'off the cuff' video and plopping it on your website or blog isn't likely to bring you a flood of new clients.

But, using video strategically can be very profitable. So... what are the best ways to use video online? Here are my favourites:

- Building rapport with existing clients and prospects.

  People like to deal with people. And video allows you to give that feel on a one-to-many basis.

- Search engines love video. The major search engines gobble up good quality video and happily make it visible for millions to see.

  The reason being that video is liked by searchers...And therefore the search engines see video as high value content for their clients.

  Even better, videos can provide high value backlinks to your site. And backlinks are one of the main influencing factors of how highly your site ranks in the search engines...

  Secret: In fact, video is often the fastest way to get a page one listing on the search engines... Ssshhh... Don't tell your competition...

- Product demonstrations, tours etc. Software providers can quickly and easily use video to demonstrate their application. Estate agents can give virtual tours of homes. Car dealers the same for cars. And many more businesses can do the same.

- Education. Whether it's showing someone how to change a light bulb, build a house or write a best man's speech, video is a very effective media for educating people.

- Selling! Video can be a very effective media for selling.

The secret to using video successfully online is to be VERY, very clear about what you are using it for.

I suggest the four main purposes to choose from are:

1. Demand generation.
2. Presentation.
3. Selling.
4. Nurturing.

For example, let's look at how you can use video for demand generation; assume we're a cosmetic dentist.

Our first step is demand generation. We distribute something that our ideal prospects will find and watch. And after they've watched our video we want them to be interested enough to head to one of our websites that offers our client magnets...

To begin, we could create a series of videos called "7 Steps to Teeth So White Your Friends Will Accuse You of Being in Beverly Hills".

We then need to distribute the videos on the internet in order people can find them i.e. put the videos on as many of the video sharing sites as we can.

And there are hundreds of them! From Youtube to Yahoo, Dailymotion, MSN, Revver and lots, lots more.

We can either submit them one by one to these sites (which takes a long time) or use one of the many video submission services around that will submit our video to multiple of these sites at once.

The most important things are to make sure:

1. Your videos have a call to action i.e. at the end you make an offer to your watcher and tell them to take a specific action in return for your client magnet. For example you may say:

   "To receive the other 6 videos head to www.blablabla.com and also receive a free tooth whitening consultation worth £75".

2. The title you enter for the video in the video sharing sites MUST be keyword rich. For example if we were a dentist in Winchester and

we wanted people to find us when they searched for "Cosmetic Dentist in Winchester" we would be very, very wise to include "Cosmetic Dentist in Winchester" in our video title...

3. You must include relevant keywords as above in the keyword section on the video sharing sites.

4. Begin your video description with a link to the site you want to point people to. This is a little known yet essential secret to getting traffic from videos.

Follow these four steps and you'll stand a great chance of your video being ranked by the search engines, your prospects finding it, enjoying it, requesting your client magnet and moving into your full follow up sequence.

Now, assuming someone has found your video and heads to your website and requests your client magnet you can then move to step 2 i.e. presentation. And your presentation could be in the form of the remaining 6 video steps, perhaps on your blog.

And you could even create a sales video to sell your services AND a follow up set of videos showing clients how to look after their teeth.

Video is a very powerful media and, for the right business, can be a real advantage in competitive differentiation, giving the ability to raise prices through expert status and increased perceived value of both your marketing process and products and services.

Exactly how you should use video in your business is not a prescription I can give here. There are too many variables for me to do that. And keep in mind video is only one piece of the puzzle and not a silver bullet.

However, I do conduct A VERY LIMITED NUMBER of in depth "Grow Your Business While You Sleep" consultations. These are for very serious business owners looking for dramatic leaps income and free time. There is a strict application process prior to acceptance into one of these consultations. To receive an application form simply head to the back of this book and follow the instructions.

If your application is successful I will work with you personally to implement everything in this book and my advanced strategies outside its scope.

---

## HOW TO APPLY FOR A "GROW YOUR BUSINESS WHILE YOUR SLEEP" CONSULTATION WITH HENRY

I will be conducting a very limited number of in depth "Grow Your Business While You Sleep" consultations. For these there is a strict application process. To request an application form head to:

**www.GrowYourBusinessWhileYouSleep.com/apply**

---

## Chapter Thirteen

# The Amazing Power of Joint Ventures

Here's something 99% of small business owners don't realise: joint ventures are one of the quickest and most cost effective ways to get new clients online or offline.

In fact, it's entirely possible you've never even considered a joint venture as a means of marketing your business.

The beauty of joint ventures is that they really are like getting something for 'nothing' – yet a 'win-win' at the same time...

Your ideal clients spend tons of money on things you don't provide. And those businesses they buy from often have a great relationship with them and have the ability to influence who they buy from.

And that spells opportunity.

Simply by building relationships with other businesses that serve the same people as you want to attract and then asking them to recommend you, you can send your profits soaring.

And on top of that, given your existing clients and prospects spend money with lots of other people then by recommending those businesses you've built relationships with you can take a slice of the money they make too!

Let's say you're an accountant and you're looking for affluent clients. You could build a relationship with the most prestigious local golf club and ask them to recommend you to their clients and in return you'll do the same for them...

You'll pick up new clients and so will they.

Now, if there isn't the opportunity to 'trade clients' you can still profit by offering other businesses products and services in return for a commission.

There really is no limit to what you can do, creativity is key.

One of the most effective ways to make joint ventures work is to monetize your email list. If you have a list of client email addresses you can arrange with a joint venture partner to email each other's lists in exchange for a commission on any products sold.

Once you've done a few of these email promotions you will get a good idea of the kind of response you will get, this is when joint ventures become really powerful.

Say you wanted to generate £1000 to buy some new equipment and you knew, based on previous joint venture promotions, you could get roughly 15-20 people out of your email list of 1000 to buy after a series of 5 emails. You'd need to choose a product or service where the commission was around £50-100 per unit and you'd have your £1000, in 5 days, on demand.

Using joint venture to create a spike in cash flow makes sense for you and your partner. And they are well within your reach...

*Chapter Fourteen*

# How to Use Information Products as Powerful Marketing Tools

Information products are one of the most powerful and underused assets a business can create.

Whether you're an accountant, hair dresser, lawyer, builder, pizza delivery boy or even, I suppose, a prostitute you undoubtedly have expertise that other people are interested in and therefore carry immense marketable value.

Let me make this even clearer by asking you a question: Why do people buy from your business?

Answer: Because you can do, or supply, things they can't by themselves.

Therefore, there is a lot of money to be made in teaching people about what you do, or even HOW to do what you do.

**I'm going to make a very bold claim here and say that every business should sell information**

## products in addition to their other products and services

The reason why is simple: it would be ridiculous not to!

Here is a list of compelling reasons to sell information products:

- Huge profit margin. For example, it can cost less than 10p to have a CD produced yet it could sell for tens, hundreds or even thousands of pounds.

- There's a huge range of products you can create. You could write a 7 page report on "How to Avoid Getting Ripped off By a Builder" and sell it for £17.

  Create a membership website about origami and sell it at £47 per month.

  Or, create a full on training course complete with 142 page manual, 6 DVD tutorials and 50 page exercise booklet on "How to Make a Six Figure Income as a Photographer" and sell it for £1997. As long as the content and marketing are good, people will buy it!

- It can take very little time to make an information product. You could write that 7 page report in an evening and even the full course could only take a month or two if you did 2 hours a day Monday to Friday!

- Provided you write about 'evergreen' topics, that is, topics that won't lose relevance with age, once you've created an info product it can pay you for life.

- They are one of the best ways to display your expertise and build trust and loyalty among your clients.

- Once you've created the sales funnel, it can run on auto-pilot and pay you a reliable, and hefty, residual income without you having to do any work.

- All the content you create can be reused and recycled into client magnets or included in any new products you create.

- There is very little regulation to worry about. Provided you don't do something silly like tell lies, make ridiculous unfounded claims or teach a profession that is regulated such as medicine or accounting without stating that your product is not a recognised qualification. Of course, you must also never plagiarise somebody else's product or work.

Now we've discussed the reasons why info products are so useful, let's move onto how you create them.

Information products can come in all shapes and sizes. The most common types are:

- eBooks
- Audio products
- Videos, including screen-capture
- Continuity (membership) websites
- Physical books, binders, CDs, DVDs etc
- Or any combination of these things

In most cases while anything physical is a bit more of a fiddle to create and distribute, not to mention more expensive, they generally have a higher perceived value. So, a DVD delivered to someone's door will have a higher perceived value than an online video and, a folder with 200 pages of information will have a higher perceived value than a PDF.

The topic of your product will, to an extent, dictate which medium is most appropriate, but in most cases you can pretty much choose whichever one you like and, in fact, there is a lot to be said for selling the same product in a couple of different mediums.

In any case, your next question is probably "how do I create these products?". So, I've broken down the process for each one below.

### How to Create an eBook to Sell

An eBook is one of the simplest products you can create.

All you need to do is create a word processed document using Microsoft Word or something similar and then turn it into a PDF file so it will be compatible with any computer. There are plenty of free programs to do this and most of them work pretty well. Having said that, the best course of action is to download a free trial of Adobe Acrobat which is the industry standard and will produce the best results.

To download the Adobe Acrobat trial just Google "adobe acrobat trial" and it should come up straight away.

The great thing about ebooks is, as with most of these media types, you can set up your website so customers can purchase and download it without any intervention from you.

## How to Create an Audio Product to Sell

Creating an audio product is easy too. All you need is a telephone and an email address. Just go to www.freeconferencecall.com and sign up. You'll get given a number to call, then you just talk down the phone and the whole thing will be recorded and emailed to you as an MP3 file.

That's it, product made!

Or, you can get a USB microphone (or a Dictaphone), some recording software and then edit it yourself.

Now, there are a few different angles you can use

with an audio product.

The three main angles for an audio product are:

The expert angle – you talk about a topic you are knowledgeable in, acting as an expert. Don't let the word expert put you off, you don't need a PhD to be an expert in something. In fact, if you've read a few books about, say, horticulture, you probably know a lot more about it than at least 75% of the population, more than enough to call yourself an 'expert'.

The reporter angle – this is similar to the expert angle, except that you are reporting about things you've observed, or have actively gone out to learn about, like a journalist. The benefit of this angle is that you are less responsible for the accuracy and quality of the content.

The interview angle – this is as it sounds, you find somebody who is knowledgeable in your chosen subject and interview them. The interviewee can be, but doesn't have to be a celebrity of some kind, even if it's just somebody known in the community. The reason you want someone well known is so you can use their popularity to help advertise your product. www.freeconferencecall.com allows two, or more, people to phone the same number and have their conversation recorded.

And it is always worth having your audio product transcribed.

## How to Create a Video Product to Sell

One of easiest types of video product to create is the screen-capture video. This medium is great for creating instructional videos, whether you use a slideshow presentation, record yourself doing something onscreen or use a combination of both people find it one of the most appealing ways to learn new things.

Videos also carry a higher perceived value than most other digitally distributed products, which enables you to sell them for more even though they take far less time to produce than, say, an eBook.

All you need is some presentation software, the most common of which is Microsoft Powerpoint, some screen-capture software and a USB microphone (find one with a good rating on Amazon.co.uk).

Screen-capture might sound complicated, but it simply does what it says on the tin, capture your screen, or in other words, record what is on your screen.

The two most common screen-capture programs are Camtasia for Microsoft Windows and Screenflow for Mac. Regardless of what program you choose, the process is exactly the same. Create a presentation, start up the screen-capture software and then record the presentation with yourself talking over the top.

You can either host the video online or produce it on DVD. To host it online you can use one of the many streaming video providers such as Ezs3.com. To produce it on DVD then you need some DVD production software. There are tons of providers. Best bet is to have a search on Google, get some free trials and make your choice from there.

Also, you can of course film live action videos with a camera or webcam if you prefer. I would suggest that in most situations there is little benefit to doing so, but the one exception would be if you were demonstrating something physical.

It is important to remember that video files are quite large and, depending on your internet connection, they can take a while to download. In light of this, it's often a good idea to split a video product into small chunks, 15-30 minutes is ideal. Of course, if you are explaining something complicated, it's reasonable to go up to an hour long.

## How to Create an Ongoing Revenue Stream With Continuity Websites

I briefly mentioned continuity websites earlier on in the book when I was talking about your 'never ending profit machine', but I'll take the time now to explain just how powerful they are.

One of the biggest causes of small business failure is lack of cash flow. The never ending profit machine is as you now know a very powerful solution to the problem.

The power of the continuity program lies in the fact that by having only a comparatively small number of members, you can reliably, and automatically, collect every penny you need to pay the bills, and probably a lot more, on the first of every month before you've done **any** work.

Just think about this for a second, you could pay all your bills and expenses on the first of every month, without fail, meaning anything else you make is pure profit. How awesome is that?!

But what I love about continuity programs, is that you can make them whatever you want them to be and one of my favourite incarnations is the continuity website.

Essentially, you create a simple website with a login system for your members and fill it with information products like the ones we've been talking about.

You can put whatever you like in there: articles, audio files, videos, even whole books you've written.

Now, whilst most continuity websites are just a conglomeration of other info products, they come in two different models: the breakage model and the usage model.

## The Breakage Model

This model is the easiest to maintain of the two, but it tends to have a greater attrition rate (the proportion of subscribers who leave each month).

It works like this: you create the website, fill it with information and then drive subscribers to it. You rarely, if ever, update the website or add new information.

The plus side to this is obvious, once you've made it, you can forget about it.

What you have to bear in mind is that because you aren't updating it people will get bored, exhaust the usefulness of the information or just forget about it and are therefore more likely to cancel their subscription quickly.

In addition, you will find that breakage continuity websites generally need to be priced low so that your members are less likely to cancel quickly. Having said that, what constitutes a low price varies depending on the industry and topic of the site, with the main differentiators being whether the site is related to making money and the affluence of your customers.

Of course, the key to finding the right price is testing, don't just pick a price out of thin air; test at least three different prices: low middle and high. You'd be surprised how elastic price can be.

NOTE: I have created numerous 'breakage' model membership sites and they've all be a pain in the proverbial wotsit. While in theory they make good sense and I do know some people doing very well with them, I have found them more trouble than they are worth. No matter how many times you tell new subscribers they are paying for access to valuable material but spread on a monthly basis - a large percentage will play dumb, cancel, ask for a refund and then go moan on forums to justify themselves despite the fact they knew what the deal was to begin with. My advice is to stick to the next model (but try these if you wish – let me know if you 'crack' them...)

## The Usage Model

This is kind of the opposite of the breakage model; rather than not pro-actively reminding people to use your site you want to encourage them to use it as much as possible.

You do this by, firstly, contacting your members often using email and secondly, adding content to your website on a regular basis (usually monthly).

Whilst this model takes more work, if done correctly, it will offer substantially lower attrition rates and can be priced higher.

The other upside is a build-up of goodwill and loyalty from your subscribers; if your content is good they will look forward to your updates and be far more likely to buy other products and services from you.

Another excellent idea is to build community features into your website so members can interact with each other and build a social circle within the site making them far less likely to cancel. Something such as a forum or message board will do nicely.

This also gives you the opportunity to interact with them yourself and build loyalty that way.

In addition to these two models of continuity, there is a third model, which is a kind of fusion of the two.

I call this model 'modular-continuity'.

The idea is simple; you deliver serialised content to your customers over a finite period of time. So, for example, you might create a 12 part course on origami and give your customers access to a new part each month for a year.

This effectively allows you to run a usage model continuity site without having to constantly produce new content, with the only downside being that customers will only ever stay for as long as the course lasts. In reality though, customers rarely stay for more than a year anyway so you don't miss out on much.

You can of course completely automate the delivery of the content and the communication with your members, making modular-continuity a very attractive model to use.

So how do you go about making a continuity site?

It's quite simple really there are lots of providers around. My favourite right now is a combination of Wordpress and something called Wishlist Member, an add on for Wordpress.

Wishlist Member allows you to protect content on

your Wordpress blog by creating membership levels. It adds a hidden page to your blog where customers can create a username and password which they can then use to log in and see your protected content.

All you have to do is send people to the sign-up page once they've paid for their membership and you're off.

To facilitate a modular-continuity site, all you have to do is create a different membership level for each piece of content and set Wishlist Member to automatically upgrade customers to the next level each month or whatever interval you choose. This is very easy to do as Wishlist Member provides an excellent, self-explanatory, interface.

In terms of actually adding content, you simply upload your articles, audio files, videos or whatever as blog posts and then set them to the relevant level of protection.

## How to Create Physical Information Products to Sell

The upside to physical products is their high perceived value; even if the content is the same, people will be far more impressed by a DVD they receive in the post than by a video online; the cost of this benefit however, is, well...cost.

Once you start delivering physical products it becomes somewhat more logistically complicated, and costly, to organise your distribution channel.

Whilst there are numerous providers who will print books and binders or duplicate CDs and DVDs, few of them deal with fulfilment too.

This can mean that for every physical product you create you either have to take the time to post the products yourself or pay a fulfilment company to do it for you. I would suggest that if you choose to sell physical information products as a side line to your main business, you should contract a fulfilment company to avoid spending all your time packing and shipping, rather than working.

What I don't want to suggest is that physical products are more hassle than they are worth, far from it – they just need a little more planning.

That basically covers the different types of information products you could create and sell. There is literally a gold mine waiting to for you to extract as much as you want...

Start thinking today about how you can integrate information products into your business.

*Chapter Fifteen*

# How to Turn Your Email Follow-Up Series Into Gold

I know I'm at risk of sounding like a stuck record but what I'm about to repeat is critical.

Remember, the first stage in our marketing system is to offer your client magnet. Typically a free report, voucher, DVD or other gift.

The purpose of our client magnet is to collect the details of prospects. Once we have their details then we move them along our sales process until they become clients.

Sometimes this will happen instantly. In many cases it'll take weeks, months and even years (many of my best clients became my subscribers as much as 3 years before spending a penny with me...).

And our primary communication vehicle for following up with our prospects and clients is email. And therefore the first emails they receive from us are of critical importance.

Now...A follow up email series is similar to writing a report.

Remember, you want people to be eager to open your emails and you want them to take action on what you reveal and click through to your website, pick up the phone, give you a call or whatever action is next in your sales process.

For that reason you need to give the whole series a 'sexy' name and you need to actually deliver consistently excellent content.

Naming your email series isn't difficult. You can follow the same kind of formula as for a special report you might give as a client magnet.

Just add the words "free email course" then the title. For example:

- 7 Insider Secrets To Hiring The Perfect Estate Agent
- Top 10 Money Saving Secrets To Installing A Pool in Your Garden
- How to Get the Maximum Price When Selling Your Car
- 9 Fatal Mistakes That Can Kill Your Home Extension Project
- 10 Most Common Mistakes Investors Make When Choosing a Stockbroker
- 5 Roadblocks That Can Stop You From Learning Greek Fast

Fundamental to designing your email series is giving some serious thought as to where your subscribers are in the buying process.

You need to think through how much your subscriber knows and what he needs to know to take the next step towards spending money with you. Think of the key information you can use to educate your subscriber and help them move forward. Again, what do you repeat to your prospects and clients over and over when you talk to them in person?

What interesting stories from your own experience or your experience working with clients can you tell to get your points across?

As email is your primary form of contact with your list it is vital that your emails are of a high quality.

The first thing you need to be clear about is what your emails are for. Whilst they are there to build rapport with your list by giving them information of value, your primary goal should always be to "sell the click".

You see, the whole purpose of each email will be to get the reader to click on a link to a website which will, ultimately, sell them something.

"Selling the click" refers to the process of convincing the reader to click on the link.

If you're a good marketer, you will provide content before you say "click here to buy my insider's guide to XYZ". This content should be original information relevant to product being sold with its own inherent value.

The question is whether you try and provide some of this information in your emails or "sell the click" and then provide the content on the web.

In general, information received in an email has the lowest perceived value out of all the media around, but that doesn't mean you should ignore the chance to provide value.

The most important thing to remember is that people are generally busy when they read emails and have a very short attention span unless you can get them out of their inbox and onto the web.

The best way to catch attention with an email, as with anything else, is a good headline. This isn't a book on copywriting but here are a few examples:

### The "Re: ..." headline

You know how when someone replies to your email it says "Re: [your subject line]"?

A great way to get people's attention is to give the appearance you are replying to them by preceding your subject line with "re:..." especially if you make it something like "Re: your question" or even better "Re: [your name] how can I XYZ?"

### The "[video update] – video name" headline

If you have a blog, or have just posted a video on a webpage, this is a great way to get people to have a look. It's best to keep the email body text really short to create some mystery, something like:

*"Hi [Customer/ProspectName],*

*I just uploaded a new video for you on XYZ.*

*Go to www.XYZ.com/video to have a look.*

*[Your name]*

*P.S. I reveal something most people wouldn't admit to, but I hope you respect me for it."*

Now let's analyse this email for the purposes of explaining email copywriting, yes, that's right, crafting emails is a science unto itself.

First things first, always write emails as if you are having a one to one conversation, never say "I have done XYZ for my loyal customers", always say "I have done XYZ for you".

There are two reasons for this.

Firstly, people like to have personal conversations; they don't like being treated as a nameless statistic i.e "just another customer or prospect".

Secondly, saying that you have done something for them invokes the unspoken rule of reciprocity, that is, if someone does something for you, you feel compelled to give something back, even if all you do is watch their video.

In addition, you should also always use the personalisation feature in your autoresponder to insert people's first name at the beginning of an email. This is very simple to do and usually involves writing something like [firstname] in place of an actual name.

The next thing to notice in the email is the P.S., one of the most effective techniques for increasing response.

This is because when people read an email, or a letter, or anything in fact, they scan it. They read the top, then the bottom and then, if it's interesting enough, the middle.

Therefore, the point of a P.S. can either be to generate intrigue and desire or simply offer another opportunity to click. In this case, because the email was so short, I used the opportunity to create some interest by saying something mysterious.

The content of what you say is largely irrelevant provided that it stands out and is true.

For instance, I could have written:

*"P.S. A lot of people won't like what I have to say, but I'm only interested in telling the truth"* and it probably would have had a similar effect.

You might think I'm telling you to be sensationalist, but I'm really not, you don't need to make up some revolutionary story or hilarious misadventure to make a P.S. effective **and** true.

The thing I wouldn't admit to for example, could simply have been that I failed to complete the London Marathon... although I didn't, I completed it twice - but you get the idea.

One final thing on the P.S., you can have as many as you like at the bottom of an email. Doing this is extremely effective, particularly if you do something like this:

*P.S. Create mystery or give a benefit*

*P.P.S. Remember the article/video/whatever is at www.XYZ.com*

As you probably guessed from the video update email, one of the best ways to get people's interest is to offer something for free, usually a client magnet.

When you're trying to "sell the click" for a client magnet one of the best things to do is repeatedly draw attention to its benefits.

Let's say you were a company selling a product on personal productivity and you'd produced a report called "7 secrets to less work and more play". The following is the benefit laden email you decide to send to people when they sign up for your report:

*Subject: [customer name] your free report on the 7 secrets to less work and more play*

*"Hi [customer name],*

*Would you like to spend less time at the office and more time at home with your spouse and kids?*

*To find out how read my report "7 secrets to less work and more play" at:*

*www.blahblhblah.com/7secrets*

*But if that doesn't interest you, let me ask you another question:*

*How much less stressed would you feel if you were able to know, with 100% certainty, that work ended at 5pm every Monday to Friday and you could just forget about it the rest of the time?*

*To learn how to make that a reality for you visit:*

*www.blahblhblah.com/7secrets*

*Best wishes,*

*[Your name]*

*P.S. I should warn you, I will be taking this report down in the very near future. The unprecedented demand is telling me this information is simply "too good" and so I intend to start charging for it as soon as I can.*

*P.P.S. the report is at*

*www.blahblhblah.com/7secrets*

Can you see how I've loaded the email with benefits by using rhetorical questions?

Because the answers to the questions are obvious, the implied benefits of reading the report are very compelling, particularly for someone who's obviously interested in this stuff because they signed up to get the report.

Can you see the other two new techniques I've snuck in there, both are in the P.S.?

Firstly, I've introduced scarcity into the equation by suggesting that I will take the report down soon. This will make people more likely to read it because our inherent fear of loss will compel them to do so.

There are all sorts of ways you can introduce scarcity into your marketing, the most common being putting a limit on how much of a particular product you sell.

You could, for example, decide to only sell 200 places in a continuity site. Obviously, you need to give a legitimate reason to avoid it sounding like a gimmick. A good, and perfectly valid, explanation could be that you only have the customer service capacity for 200 members.

The second technique I used was social proof. By mentioning the "unprecedented demand" I'm implying the information is considered desirable by a lot of other people and this can only make it more desirable for whoever reads the email.

One thing you should never underestimate is the power of the special offer, especially where email marketing is concerned.

One of the best ways to grab a nice injection of cash is to run a sale... Such as a 25% discount, or even a half-price sale, on notable dates on the calendar like Easter, Halloween, Christmas and Valentine's Day. You can even do impromptu sales if you feel like it; "because I appreciate you" sales go down very well.

We're coming to the end of the section on email marketing; however, I have one last piece of advice for you:

### Answer your emails

As time consuming and annoying as it might be, answering client queries is one of the most effective ways to boost sales and build the kind of relationships that lead to repeat customers.

The truth is, when people send you a silly question, they are often just looking for a final bit of reassurance before they commit to purchase. Of course, there are some timewasters but you can simply remove them from your email list.

The quicker you can respond to emails the better; the maximum a customer should have to wait for a response is 24 hours.

Obviously, answering emails is not your top priority and it shouldn't be, but that doesn't mean it isn't important. Where possible try and find a few 10-15 minute slots during the day to answer emails, or, if you have one, get your receptionist to do it.

## Chapter Sixteen

# How to Use Social Media for Profit

Do you remember back in the mid to late 90s when the internet was really starting to 'kick off' and people were going crazy about the possibilities?

Well, we are in a similar situation now, except this time the fuss isn't about the internet, but about social media.

Sites like Facebook and Twitter are exploding and it's impossible to underestimate what the 'social media revolution' they are leading is going to do for business.

In truth, at the moment the impact these sites will have on your business can be limited.

There are over 500 million users on Facebook at the time I'm writing this book and around half of them spend an average of 1 hour a day on the site. That is unprecedented, beyond anything that's happened before.

**Moreover, Facebook is soon set to overtake even Google in advertising revenue, making it something you simply cannot afford to ignore as a**

## local business

From your perspective as a business owner, Facebook is simultaneously a paid advertising network and a free advertising network.

Not only can you serve people highly targeted ads based on demographic data like age, address, occupation and marital status but also their tastes in anything from films, music and videogames, to food, leisure activities, favourite celebrity and even political ideology or religion.

In the next few years we will start to experience nothing short of a revolution in advertising where people will interact directly, probably via Facebook, with the businesses they use. You will be able to have an individual relationship with every single one of your customers.

Let me put this into perspective; for years Tesco have been using their loyalty card scheme to work towards what seemed like an impossible goal: to build a database of demographic data on every single UK citizen.

It looks very likely, if not inevitable, that Facebook will beat them to it in the next few years and the site was only founded in February 2004!

However, whilst I'm sure this all seems rather exciting, I suspect you're still wondering how you can make social media work for your business NOW.

Well, the obvious place to start is paying for advertisements on Facebook to send people in your local area who are interested in what you provide to your new website. This is only the tip of the iceberg though!

### The real power of social media is twofold: viral spread and social proof

Facebook allows business owners like you to create what they call "fan pages". Essentially, these are a Facebook profile for your business, complete with a wall to write things on, an info page and many other things besides.

The reason it's called a fan page is because people can 'like' it by clicking a little button that says "like". When somebody 'likes' a page an update is sent to all their friends saying "so and so likes blah blah blah" and also the fact they like it is recorded on their info page forevermore. This creates instant viral spread.

So, if you create a Facebook fan page for your business you can immediately start building a viral list of people who like you.

Also, anybody who looks at your fan page can see how many people like you, the more people like you, the more popular your business becomes and the greater social proof it will exert.

The best bit about all this though, is that when somebody likes your page, they are implicitly giving you permission to contact them because anything you write on your 'wall' will appear on their list of updates.

The possibilities are endless!

I'm sure this all seems rather confusing so I'm going to go all out and give you my 'Facebook Domination Formula'.

What I'm going to suggest you do is something that pretty much nobody has picked up on yet. You're going to fuse Facebook with the list building techniques in this book by:

**Literally copying your client magnet capture site and pasting it onto a Facebook fan page dedicated to your business**

Very few people have yet to spot this huge opportunity. Facebook has a built in function that allows you to create a webpage within your fan page meaning you can collect email address in exchange for client magnets just as you would on your normal website.

Actually building a fan page requires no more technical knowledge than you need to sign up for a normal Facebook account and that is pretty much zero. All you need to do is go to www.facebook.com and click on the link that says "create a page for a celebrity, band or business" then follow the simple instructions.

Once it's built, you simply need to add a new tab to your fan page and then choose the "FBML" (Facebook's version of HTML) type and you'll be presented with an empty text box. All you have to do is copy the code from your website into the box and press ok (note: Facebook is changing all the time. This is the case at the time of writing this book. The specifics of how to do this may change but the strategy will not).

HEY PRESTO!

You have a single action website to deliver your client magnets - within your Facebook fan page.

The next step is to go into the options for your fan page and set it so that:

A. People can only see the content on the page after they've liked it and...

B. When someone likes it they are sent straight to your lead generation page.

Now you've set it up all you have to do is start the snowball of business groupies rolling until it becomes self-sustaining and turns into an avalanche.

The process for doing this is simple but requires a little education in social dynamics and, I suppose, maths for it to make sense.

What you need to do is find people who are interested in what you offer, but who also know a lot of other people who are interested in it too. This is to facilitate viral spread in a cost effective way.

To explain this I'm going to have to get a bit fancy pants so bear with me. Let's say you're a business selling comics.

You know you can use Facebook to serve ads to people who are interested in comics, that's easy, but you also know that there are different demographic groups interested in comic books. Members of some groups, like the 14-17 year old boys group, are likely to know a lot of other comic book geeks, whilst other groups are less likely to know other geeks.

As a stereotypical comic book geek yourself, your pretty good at maths and you know a thing or two about how viral spread works.

Say we look at Dave, a guy who LOVES comics and frequents your store "Comic Book Heaven Southampton". If he liked your Facebook fan page then all his 1053 friends on the site would see an update saying "Dave Smith likes Comic Book Heaven Southampton".

The higher the number of people in those 1053 friends who like comic books, the higher the number of viral likes you are going to get as a result of Dave liking your page, and therefore, the more cost effective your advertising will be.

In other words, when you're deciding who to serve ads to on Facebook you want to look for demographics with a high density of people interested in what you sell.

As a side note, unless you serve people all over the country (or world), make sure you only advertise to people in your area.

That's the general rule, now we're going to talk specifics.

I'm going to suggest either a two or three-pronged attack depending on how much time you, or your employees, have to build your Facebook following.

I'll start with the two compulsory strategies and finish with the optional one.

The first, and simplest, is to utilise word of mouth.

Login to your personal Facebook account, if you don't have one make one, not just for business purposes, but because it's awesome!

Once you're in, search for your new business fan page and like it. Then go to the fan page, you should see an option (on the left) to suggest the page to your friends, choose all of them (or maybe just those in the local area) and click ok.

**Now, whenever you see or talk to someone you're friends with on Facebook say:**

*"Oh, by the way, I've started up a fan page for my business, any chance you could like it and suggest it to your friends; you get a free report / voucher /*

*video / kitten / cup cake whatever for signing up and I'd really appreciate it. Thanks again."*

And perhaps more importantly, do exactly the same thing with your customers!

You should start to see your following rise quite quickly if you're intense enough about it.

### Strategy number two is about buying highly targeted paid adverts on Facebook

To find Facebook's advertising platform, just login to your fan page, scroll to the bottom and you should see a link that just says "advertising". Just follow the instructions it gives you to set up an account.

This book isn't the place for analysis of how to write adverts or structure a pay per click campaign. But targeting people on Facebook is completely different to most other advertising networks like Google Adwords, Yahoo and MSN.

Although Facebook does use keywords to target people, you put keywords in specific categories like occupation, activities or interests.

In addition, Facebook is very cleverly going through all the keywords in these categories and giving them their own page. This is great for advertisers like you because you can see exactly how many people are, for example, dental technicians or how many people like comic books.

What you'll need to do is define a number of demographic groups that are likely to have a high density of people interested in your wares and then create an ad for each one.

The best way to do this is through Facebook fan pages and groups. By finding Facebook fan pages and groups with interests related to what you sell you can then target users based on their affiliation with those fan pages and groups.

For example, if you were a business selling craft supplies you would target people in your local area who were affiliated with fan pages related to crafts in general, or specific crafts, like knitting or painting.

It is important to be as specific as possible with your targeting because not only are you more likely to find the right people, but the more specific you are, the less competition you have for advertising space meaning the cost goes down significantly.

The third strategy is very much related to the second, but a bit more labour intensive. Rather than just serving ads to these fan pages and groups, you're going to actively reach out to them in person.

You can do this yourself, ask your employees to do it or both.

Let's go back to the craft shop example. Using a personal Facebook profile, either yours or an employee's, you could like the page "Craft Addicts

Southampton" and start interacting with it.

You want to find pages that are quite active with people interacting socially a lot on them. This tends to be truer for smaller pages. In these cases you will want to find the page's 'regulars', especially its administrators, and start commenting on their posts as well as posting your own insightful tip bits about crafts.

Once you've built a relationship with them you can mention your fan page and the free gift people get if they like it and ask them to write a post about it on their fan page.

I should point out that because of the large time investment needed; it is only worth doing this for extremely well targeted and active fan pages and groups. This is not to suggest that the strategy is not effective, if done correctly it can be extremely so.

The final thing you need to know about Facebook is how to interact with your new fan page following.

Your primary concern should be to make sure your posts are interesting and NOT spam.

In general, you want to post about:

- Special offers – you can give a website link where people can give their email address in exchange for a promotional code.

- Interesting tip bits of information to do with your business niche. For example, if you were the owner of that comic book store you could mention a new series of comics that has just come out. Or, if you're a hairdresser you could give a short piece of advice on styling your hair.

- Entice people by offering other client magnets in exchange for their email address.

Social media is still 'new' and how it will develop is still unclear.

What I can tell you for sure is this. Just like when the telephone first arrived, when the first computer arrives, when the fax machine arrived, when the internet arrived, it does change things. BUT, it is ONLY another piece of your communication funnel - your client gathering and nurturing opportunities.

It will never be the 'magic bullet' – don't be fooled into thinking it will be...

## Chapter Seventeen

# The Viral Power of the Internet

One of the biggest secrets to rapid business growth online and offline is getting "word of mouth" business or referrals from happy clients and prospects.

And the internet is an ideal medium for generating referrals quickly and consistently.

However, for most businesses these are few and far between.

Why?

Well... Rarely is it due to the fact their clients don't want to refer them – but rather, it's just not made easy enough for them to do so...

The biggest mistake most business owners make is not making it dead easy for their prospects and clients to recommend them.

If you want to get a steady stream of high quality prospects recommended to you, you need to create multiple, effective referral systems.

Here are a few very simple systems you can implement in your online marketing.

First whenever you send an email make sure you include a note about at least one of your client magnets AND a link to the website where readers can get it. For example if we were an estate agent we may include a note at the bottom of all your emails saying:

*"FREE Report Reveals 7 Secrets to Selling Your Home Quickly and For Maximum Price. To claim your free report head to www.blablabla.com."*

You'll be astonished how often your emails are forwarded to friends and associates by the recipient. Just including a note like this at the end of your emails can generate new prospects and clients for years.

Now, if when you send an email which contains high quality content or leads to high quality content on your website or a special offer seriously consider adding one simple line:

*"You are welcome to share this valuable content with your friends. Just forward them this email."*

Change the wording to be more specific about the information each email leads to and the specific type of people they know that might benefit.

You can also get visitors to your site to recommend it to their friends and associates using a "Tell A Friend" script OR what is now even more powerful – post a link to their social networking pages such as Facebook, Myspace and Twitter.

Let's start with a tell a friend script. You've probably seen tell a friend scripts and there's a good chance you've even used one without really thinking about the viral marketing implications.

The script is simple.

A visitor to your site sees a box that says something like "Tell your friends about this site" or "Tell your friends about this web page" or "Tell your friends about this free report".

Your visitor enters his name and the names and email addresses of a few of his friends.

The script sends an email to those friends on your visitor's behalf recommending your site or your web page or your free report.

The real power of a tell a friend script is in making it dead easy for visitors to your site to pass on the word.

You can make your tell a friend scripts even more powerful by giving a valuable gift i.e. another client magnet such as a report, eBook, discount voucher or audio to people who refer a certain number of their friends to your site.

Now, the process with social networking sites is

very similar. For example, it is now very easy to add a Facebook 'LIKE' button to every post on your blog. That means if someone likes your post they can simply click the 'like' button and share it with their friends on Facebook.

If their friends also like the link then they can share it with their friends and on and on. This is a very simple yet powerful 'viral' opportunity.

To really capitalise on the viral nature of social networks however, you do need to have a deliberate plan to make your post or site worthy of a viral spread. A pretty in depth process and outside the scope of this book but something I'm willing to help the right clients with.

You can also turn your site into a viral machine by paying for your clients to send you visitors.

How?

### Pay Affiliates to Promote Your Site, Products and Services

While many of your visitors, subscribers and clients will be happy to pass on your free content and recommend it to others in many cases you can create many times the viral effect by paying for the sales they send you online.

How do you do that?

In a similar vain to joint ventures we recruit what we call in the online world 'affiliates'.

These are people you pay a certain commission to when certain a thing occurs through their making.

That could be a sale of a product, a prospect signing up for one of your client magnets or in some cases even just a click on a specific website 'link'.

This is like having a whole army of commissioned sales people out making money while they promote your products and services.

## You Can Even Charge for
## Client magnets

Someone who has requested one of your client magnets for free is usually NOT as good prospect as someone who has paid their own money for one.

For example, if you are an accountant and you offer a report "101 Little Known Ways to Reduce Your Tax Bill by as Much as Half", you could charge a fee for the report.

People that pay for the report have immediately put a higher value on your expertise than someone who received it free. So there's a good argument to be made for selling some of your client magnets as actual products instead of giving them away free.

And if you're selling those client magnets that

means you can also give commissions.

Remember the whole point of a client magnet is to build a powerful list of prospects and clients you can sell back end products and services to. So it's just plain common sense to be as generous to your affiliates as possible giving up to 100% commissions on your client magnet products.

And giving generous commissions combined with an online sales letter that converts a high percentage of visitors to buyers can have a huge viral effect.

## But Note This

As I've just outlined you can charge for some of your client magnets and in most situations you should. But be aware that your demand generation 'machine' is governed by a 'virtual' set of dials that can be turned up or down.

If you put a price on your client magnets you'll turn up the price dial and in turn reduce the number of prospects you collect.

The more you turn the dial up, the fewer prospects you'll amass and therefore the less people you'll have to communicate with automatically via email and sell your products and services.

However, these prospects will in most cases be much better quality.

## But it's not that simple.

IF the majority of your follow up sequence is email then because that is nigh on free it is my recommendation that you look for the MAXIMUM volume of prospects requesting your client magnet.

Why?

Because it'll cost you no more to send 5,000 emails than it will send 500 and there is a good chance there will be buyers in the extra 4,500...

A more advanced strategy is to offer free client magnets to begin with and then filter your prospect list into specific interest groups based on their request for additional client magnets that may or may not cost money...

We're beginning to get more advanced here and at this stage it's something to be thinking about but not overly concerned with.

To begin you should just MAKE SURE you are utilizing every possible opportunity you can find to collect the details of people who are ideal clients for you by offering your client magnets in as many different ways as you can...

Build the biggest list of ideal clients as you can.

You can mine that list for years and years and

years... As long as you treat them as they deserve (like you'd like to be treated yourself... well).

*Chapter Eighteen*

# This All Sounds Great But I'm a Local Business in a Local Town and my Clients are Tourists!

Everything we've covered so far is applicable to any size business in any size village town or city – even if the economy there is driven by tourists.

And that can seem like a good excuse for not building an email list. Tourists aren't in town for long and then they're back off home. On the outside that seems a logical argument.

But, when I hear a business relies on tourists my first thought is 'BINGO' and then 'collecting prospect and client details is even more critical' than with a non tourist led business.

Why?

Well, those people that come see you, spend money

with you then go home spend piles of money on other things.

In fact, if you could just extract a tiny percentage of their other spend you'd be set up for life. And the first step to doing that is to find out who they are, and get permission to contact them.

There is absolutely no way you'll sell them anything once they go home if you don't collect their details and yet if you do there are endless ways to sell them things they would normally buy from others... AND, by keeping in contact with them they're much more likely to come back and see you again!

So, if this applies to you, drop the excuses and let's go look at some real strategies you can use.

First, if for example you own a restaurant you can often increase your turnover and profits substantially by offering gifts to your patrons. Give your tourist diners a gift voucher worth say £5, £10, £20 or more (depending on the average price of your meals). But rather than have an expiry date a few weeks in advance, have the voucher expire within 48 hours.

Following a long day shopping, walking, site-seeing or just having fun, it can be a real effort to choose which restaurant to visit.

As long as you served them well previously, by offering them a free gift voucher it is very likely they'll come back and spend a lot more than the value of the voucher...

And the same principle applies for tour operators and other types of businesses where you offer products and services tourists can use or can use more than once during their visit to your town or city.

You can also joint venture with other businesses serving the same clients and cross promote each other's restaurants, tours, hire facilities etc. with your clients and prospects.

As you've gone to all the trouble and expense of getting a client and giving them exceptional service, you want to make sure they continue to get service from the best businesses in your area...the businesses you recommend.

And you want to maximize the profits you make from every transaction you have with your clients.

### So Why Should You Build An Email List?

Well, beyond what you can offer them while they're actually in your area there are ENDLESS things you can offer them when they go home and when they return and in fact wherever they are in the world.

And collecting their email details is vital.

It used to be that when a tourist went home in most cases it became cost prohibitive to send them direct mail in order to sell them other peoples products and services from which you receive a commission.

BUT, email reduces that cost to almost ZERO and means you can offer an endless array of products and services at almost no cost and in turn make more profits!

And you know a lot more about the tourists that have visited you than may first meet the eye. If you've done a good job of collecting not just email but address details and other lifestyle info too then you can very carefully pick your products and service which match their demographics and therefore are likely to be of interest to them.

For example – if they've flown to you from another country you know they buy air travel then there are tons of travel sites that will happily pay you a commission for referring your clients to them.

All you need do is join their affiliate program, then send your clients and prospects an email with a compelling reason to click on your affiliate link to be taken to the travel companies site. Dependent on what affiliate arrangement you have you may get commission for any subsequent sales, people who request more information or in some cases even just people that click on your link!

There's a good chance they'll be interested in travel guides, and even eBooks, reports, books on how to save money on travel and find the best destinations.

The options are limitless. And this is important.

ANY commission you make here is almost entirely PROFIT you would not normally have seen.

It costs almost nothing to collect contact details and almost nothing to send your emails!

## And It Doesn't End There
## Tourists Can Be A Source Of High Quality Referrals

Also, many of your clients will have friends who also travel and they'll be happy to recommend your business.

You can send your clients an email with a gift voucher of some kind and tell them they can use it themselves if they're ever back in your area again or they can pass it on to a friend.

The real key here is to think beyond what you can offer to a single client.

Your clients buy a whole range of products and services and they have a huge network of friends, work mates and associates. Just by capturing contact details and following up you have instant access to that potential gold mine.

## *Chapter Nineteen*

# Can These Two Numbers Change Your Life?

Back in the 1800's if you wanted to start a business your options were much more limited than they are now. You could become a carpenter, baker, butcher, jeweller or start any number of other businesses.

You'd set up your business – get yourself some premises. But how would you make money?

Well, simply by providing something of value to your customers they in turn would reward you with money.

But how would you find your customers?

There was no postal service, no internet, few sign writers and little if any opportunity for publicity. International business was extremely limited and often dangerous...

Competition did exist. If another cobbler set up in the same village then you would either lose a big chunk of your business or else you'd have to get 'rid' of them.

Yet many individuals and many business owners managed to amass wealth. That simple transaction of money in return for value has not changed. And that value exchange can be many things. It can be goods, services, problem solutions or numerous other things.

And the fundamental ingredients are simple.

1. You need something to sell.
2. You need a supply of people willing and able to give you money.

And it doesn't matter in which order those two things are created. If you have a good product, it's useless unless you have a constant stream of people able to buy it.

If you know where to tap into a constant stream of people who are willing and able to buy something then you can easily create that thing they wish to buy.

What's important is that one of those two things IS way more important than the other.

And that's the constant stream of people who have the ability and want to exchange money for what you have.

That is the simple essence of ALL commerce. It is NO more complicated than that.

So...Assuming you have something of value to exchange with people for money, all you need to do is:

1.  Find more of those people who want what you have.
2.  Get them buying more from you, more often.

And that's the end of this book.

Do those two things and you can amass as much wealth, fame and envy as you wish. BUT, you and I both know it's not quite that simple.

It's not a lot more complicated, but there is ONE more dynamic you need to consider.

### And it's this part that gets people's knickers in a real twist

It's no good just exchanging something for money. You MUST exchange something for MORE money that it cost you to make it, deliver it and market it. That extra money is your profit.

And PROFIT is the ONLY reason to be in business. Without profit you might as well GIVE up and go get a job.

You see, it DOES cost you SOMETHING to acquire a new customer.

Whether that is the cost of an ad, the cost of a telephone call, the cost of a meeting and or any other combination of things you do to get that customer to BUY something from you in the first place.

And it also DOES cost you something to deliver whatever it is you sell them; whether that is a 'widget', a thing, a service or some of your time.

But there's more good news buried in here (or at least there should be and if there's not we'll fix it).

In most cases a customer will buy from you more than once.

It's rare we visit hairdressers once.

It's rare we buy a new car and don't go back there for a service.

It's rare we take something to the dry cleaners and don't go back again.

It's rare we only go to a supermarket once.

It's rare we only go to a dentist once.

And that means your AVERAGE customer is worth a lot more to you than that first, initial, purchase...

So we've got two new crucial dynamics here.

1. How much it costs you to acquire a new customer.

2. How much your average customer is worth to you in profits over their lifetime.

Take a second to let that sink in. Re-read it and think. Within those two sentences lies the path to unlimited growth in your business. Let's look at an example.

Say we're a beauty salon in a small town. We've decided to use the Yellow Pages to market our salon.

The ad costs us £1,000 for a year.

Over the year it generates us 100 new customers.

That means our average cost to acquire a new customer via the Yellow Pages is £10.

And we've looked back at our customer records and discovered on average a customer stays with us for 18 months and spends a total of £360.

With our overheads removed at our current level of business that means we make a profit of £212 on average per new customer.

Remember, it cost us £10 to acquire that new customer.

That means the Yellow Pages has made us £202 per customer or we've turned every £10 we spent in the Yellow Pages into £202!

Pretty good deal right.

Trouble is it only generated up 100 new customers and that's not nearly enough.

So, we decide to run a direct mail piece.

We're going to send a letter to 5,000 targeted people in our local area and invite them to come see us in the salon.

By the time we've paid for printing and postage the mail drop is going to cost us £3,000.

We send out the mail and get a 1% response. That's 30 new customers.

That means each customer cost us £100! Ouch...

And on top of that on average the first time people visit they only spend £30!!!

That means we've lost £70 on the first visit of each new customer!!!

Woops...

Our mailing has failed. And most people would NEVER mail again... BUT...

Remember – our average lifetime customer profit is £212.

That means over time those 30 customers will be worth £6,360!

We've just turned our £3,000 mailing into over £6,360!

That means if we have another 100,000 quality people we could mail we could generate over another £127,200!

See how important these numbers are?

They are the keys to opening the vault to all the success you need.

Now of course, NOT all the marketing you do will work this well. And I have of course plucked all these numbers out of thin air.

But the principle remains the same.

Once you KNOW with certainty how much profit the average customer makes you and TRACK how much it costs you to acquire a new customer, your options are infinite.

If you take NOTHING else form this book – spending your time understanding these two numbers will do more to catapult your success than anything else.

Because so few business owners even know these numbers exist you now have in your hands an enormous competitive advantage 'CLUB' you can use to beat your competition over the head for years.

Enjoy it ------ and use it wisely...

*Chapter Twenty*

# The Transformation Checklist

We've covered a huge amount of strategies and tactics. None are hard; all can have a profound impact on your business.

What follows now is a definitive collection of all the steps you can take to get results NOW.

I suggest you go through it and put a tick or a cross next to each point so you know exactly what you need to do to grow your business while you sleep.

1. Are you creating 'MADNESS'. i.e. are you offering your client magnets to the marketplace via as many different media as possible (online AND offline)?

2. Are you capturing the names, email addresses and other details of your prospects and clients in return for your client magnets?

3. Do you have single action websites in place offering your client magnets in return for prospects detail?

4. Are you following up with your list of prospects and clients using:

    a.    Email autoresponders?
    b.    SMS (text) messages?
    c.    Direct mail e.g. postcards, letters?
    d.    Voice broadcast?

5. Do you have your 'Never Ending Profit Machine' in place with a proper marketing funnel, so you can generate consistent residual income?

6. Do you have a viral marketing plan utilizing joint ventures, client referrals and social media?

7. Are you adding EVERY prospect and customer you come into contact with into your lead generation funnel, whether in person, by phone, email or anything?

8. Do you have an email sign up form on your website, Facebook fan page and blog?

9. Are you using highly targeted client magnets such as reports, consultations, gift vouchers and prizes as an incentive to get people to sign up to your email list?

10. Are you collecting as much data as possible about your prospects and clients including addresses and phone numbers?

11. Are you using time restraints on claiming your client magnets and on your gift vouchers as an incentive for prospects and clients to act NOW?

12. Do all your client magnets and other lead generation offers have back end offers designed to maximise your profit?

13. Have you included an offer for a client magnet on the back of your business cards?

14. Are you giving business cards to all your employees so they can distribute them to people they meet?

15. Do you have VIP cards for possible high value clients offering an extra special client magnet?

16. Do you regularly add new, highly targeted, high quality content to your website optimized for valuable long tail keywords?

17. Do you have a blog which you update regularly for the purposes of both search engine optimization and delivering high quality content?

18. As part of your viral marketing plan, do you regularly post on other blogs, forums and Facebook pages?

19. Do you utilize ebay as another means of selling your products and services?

20. Do you make use of free online classified ads to sell your products and services?

21. Do you have pay per click advertising campaigns on Google Adwords, Yahoo, Bing and Facebook?

22. Are you optimizing your pay per click campaigns using split testing and tracking?

23. Do you collect testimonials from clients and make use of them in your marketing?

24. Do the images on your website have file names that match your keywords phrases to aid in search engine and pay per click optimization?

25. Do all your images have captions that both emphasize your marketing message and contain your keywords to help search engine optimization?

26. Do you have a video marketing strategy including lead generation videos on sites like Youtube, DaliyMotion and Revver?

27. Have you set up joint ventures with other businesses to help promote your products and services?

28. Do you have an ascension model, that is, a progressively more expensive funnel of products and services (including information products) through which to guide your clients as they gain trust in you?

29. Do you use online sales letters (including video sales letters) as a means of selling to your prospects and clients?

30. Are you using email follow up sequences to direct

your prospects and clients to your client magnets and offers?

31.  Are you encouraging your prospects and clients to get their friends and family to sign up to get your client magnets?

32. Are you distributing your client magnets using 'tell a friend' scripts on your website?

33. Have you added the Facebook 'like' button to all your webpages, blog pages and single action websites?

34. Do you have a paid affiliate program for prospects, clients and joint venture partners who distribute your client magnets?

35. Are you following up with key prospects, clients and joint venture partners in person, whether by email, letter or phone?

36. Are you answering all your business emails within 15 minutes, or at the very least, twice a day?

37. Do you have pre-defined and automatically delivered special offers and promotions for special dates and holidays like Easter, Christmas, New Year, Halloween and client birthdays utilising email, direct mail, SMS messaging and voice broadcast?

38. Are you acting as an affiliate yourself promoting

other people's products and services to your list in exchange for a commission?

39. Are you constantly revising and revisiting your marketing in order to find ways to improve it through both brainstorming and consistent testing and evaluation of things like your sales messages and pay per click campaigns?

40. Are you making sure you direct the vast majority of your attention to the 20% of your marketing that is getting the results and automating the remaining 80%?

## Chapter Twenty One

# How to Avoid Overwhelm

If you've just run through the 40 point checklist then right now I suspect you'll be feeling a little overwhelmed.

Maybe even a little confused, anxious and stressed about where to start.

You'd hoped this book would show you how to grow your business in your sleep.

And you'd hope that would be as easy as ordering a pizza, but in the back of your mind you had a feeling it might take some work.

The bad news is there are no shortcuts to success and as the saying goes 'nothing worth doing is ever easy'. You do have to take action and do SOMETHING to make this work for your business.

But it's well worth it in terms of money, time and peace of mind.

The good news is that you do not have to do it all.

There are loads of companies around to help you.

From building websites to providing your autoresponder, SEO services and lots, lots more.

But keep in mind that just like when websites were first 'new' this isn't as simple as 'just doing it'. It requires a lot more experience and understanding of what really works, and what really doesn't work, to actually make a difference to your business.

Beware of anyone that claims to have the 'magic bullet', 'the secret' – I know, and I'm sure you do to, that such a thing doesn't actually exist.

But my vision is to make this easy.

To do it all for you – so you can focus on what you do best: creating products and services and serving your clients.

**And we can do it all for --- *FAST***

Having my team and I implement and integrated online and offline marketing system, execute it and maintain is of course the easiest way to grow your business while you sleep.

And as I'm sure you now appreciate, integrating profitable online marketing into your business involves a heck of a lot more than a bit of SEO work or a few tweaks to your website. Sure those things will help but there's a much bigger opportunity than that and not taking advantage of it is something you'll likely regret.

But we won't help just anyone. I've spent too many years working for people I didn't like.

To work with me directly there is a strict application process. You are welcome to request an application form via the instructions at the back of this book or head to:

www.GrowYourBusinessWhileYouSleep.com/apply

No promises.

*Chapter Twenty Two*

# The Key to the Kingdom

As I finish writing this book we're tentatively emerging from an unprecedented downturn in economic events.

Economies the world over buckled and Governments ploughed hundreds of billions of pounds into supporting their financial systems. Times have been tough for many.

It's my perhaps 'ignorant' assertion that economic uncertainty is a self-perpetuating phenomenon. Yes, everything in the world runs in cycles; from our climate, to war and peace, to the economy.

But, as soon as there is even one little 'sniff' of a downturn in the housing market, exports, a rise in inflation or a rise in food prices, the media gobbles it up and chucks it out into our society with such force and consistency, it is nigh on impossible to be unaffected.

And at some psychological level it has an effect on all of us. For most the effect is to create worry, uncertainty and a tightening of wallets and purses. That in turn fuels the challenge itself creating more 'food' for the media and the self-perpetuation begins.

The reality is that money does not disappear. When times are tough for some, others are having their best times ever.

**Money simply flows, it moves from place to place. It has no regard for to whom it goes or from whom it came.**

It cares not whether it is exchanged as a gift to a local church, a birthday present for a friend, weapons of mass destruction or in return for pornography. It has no morals and it has no favourites.

We live in an affluent society, we live in affluent times. There is more money flowing between people and businesses everyday than any of us could possibly spend in a lifetime.

What will separate those who survive, those who thrive and those who crumble in so called "economically uncertain times" is little dependent on the product or service being 'peddled' and much more dependent on the skill of the 'peddler' in finding and showing the people with money in their pockets how they can help them.

That is your job.

That is your only job.

The most vulnerable businesses are the ones who

bury their heads in the sand, batten down the hatches and just 'hope for the best'.

For those who embrace the challenge of finding and serving those with money, the potential rewards are higher than ever before.

It's easy to make money and be successful in good times, anyone with an ounce of business aptitude can succeed – and we've all been lucky enough to enjoy good times for years. But, when things start to turn and the 'easy' money is gone, only those with their wits about them, those willing to improve their skills, experiment, change and progress will succeed...

And remember, 'while the cats away' and your competition holds onto the purse strings... 'The mouse CAN play'...Yes, when times are tough, there are less people in the 'game' and your chances of winning are higher...

The strategies you've discover in this book will help you win more consistently than ever.

For the average small business owner there are more opportunities to serve more people at less cost and more profit than there ever have been.

And the internet plays a critical role in making that so.

**Remember**

We started this book talking about my father's vision back in 1989.

How one day we'd be able to get any music and any video at anytime, anywhere in the world from 'up above'.

Back then I had to hold back the laughter.

Nowadays his vision is just 'normal'.

But think for a moment how much has changed in the last two hundred years. Not just in technology terms but in society, beliefs and our values.

The world is changing fast and I suspect that pace of change will only increase.

And that means your strategies, my strategies and our competitors strategies must change – they have to as markets change.

The way we do business today is almost unrecognizably different to even as little as 30 years ago.

And for sure, the internet and the way we use it to do business will change too...you can absolutely rely on that.

But as we discussed right back at the start of this book, there is one principle that will never change.

## Business is simply the exchange of value for money

Nothing more complicated than that.

And value is in the eye of the beholder.

Yes, PEOPLE.

Your prospects, your clients.

For all the great advances in technology, the endless new opportunities that present to us every day, the 'gizmos' that save us time and the adventures that distract us, ultimately, how successful you and I become is down to how many people to whom we can give value.

And gaining an intimate knowledge of your prospects and clients is the greatest secret you will ever discover.

The moment you switch from just another provider of what you do to being 100%, completely, hand on heart focused on improving other people's lives...You can achieve whatever success you want.

Spend time listening to your prospects and clients. Find out what they really want, what they need.

Find out what keeps them awake at night, what gets them up in the morning, what makes their day the best day ever?

Find out why they choose to buy from you and not from someone else?

When you take the time to really get to know the people you do business with and the people you hope to do business with you will always have your finger on the pulse of the market.

And you'll always be one step ahead of the crowd.

The average business in your category is just that 'average'.

And there's nothing special about being average.

When you take that extra step and dig deep into your prospects and clients wants, needs and desires you'll know with almost pinpoint accuracy how to pre-educate and follow-up with them so you become the ONLY natural provider of what you do for them.

And you'll easily be able to take advantages of new technologies, new markets, and uncover a whole new world of opportunities.

However your business develops, however the world changes, the core of every successful business is the same... Adding value to living, breathing, loving people's lives... People just like you with desires, aspirations, challenges, opportunities, happiness and sadness.

So get out there today, take what you've learned in

this book and take action, change people's lives and make the world a better place.

Time for me to have a nice cup of earl grey tea and a bicuit.

Thanks for reading, good luck and I hope to meet you soon.

Your friend, Henry.

P.S. Now head to the last few pages in this book and follow the instructions to claim your freebies. They won't be available forever... ☺

P.P.S. On the next page there is a bonus chapter. It's a bit weird...

# Self-Indulgent 'Psycho-Babble' or the Ultimate Secret to Success?

"There is a magnet in your heart that will attract true friends. That magnet is unselfishness, thinking of others first... when you learn to live for others, they will live for you."

- Paramahansa Yogananda (1893–1952)

# *WARNING:*

# What You're About to Discover Pierces Right to the Very Core of Human Nature.

# It Can Be Used to Do 'BAD' Things.

# PLEASE Only Use It for GOOD!

My early career as a salesman had me leading a double life.

On the outside I was expected to be a confident, assertive, persuasive, deal making 'demon'. But on the inside I was shy, semi-reclusive, self-proclaimed comedian who was desperately looking for a way to escape.

For years I was literally teetering on the edge of insanity.

Was my whole life a 'lie'?

The big house (with big mortgage), the flashy sports car and the endless electronic gadgets were meaningless in comparison to the dread that would build inside me every Sunday evening.

It wasn't as if I'd been tricked into the career I was in.

I chose it.

Quite why I'm not sure.

But there I was – apparently stuck. And there I stayed for many years.

In the end I escaped by default. As I described in the introduction, another redundancy forced me to get on with something new. And making that a success was, I believe, down to a simple exercise I'll reveal in a minute.

But I was left intrigued.

Intrigued at how I'd got myself into my early 'pickle' and how perhaps my experience could help others suffering from the same.

It wasn't as if I was the only one.

I knew for a fact that about 90% of the people in every company I'd ever worked for would rather have been doing something else.

And it wasn't just about work. Home lives were just as troublesome.

It seemed that most people are like this:

OUTER PERSON
*(what the world sees)*

INNER PERSON
*(the real you)*

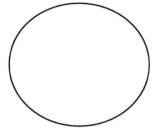

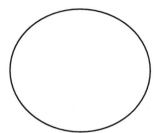

This is the person we project to the World. The person we think we should be. The person others want us to be.

This is the person we truly are inside.

## The Outer You

The outer person is the person we've been conditioned to project to the world.

The person we think we should be.

The person others want us to be.

The person we think we need to be to fit in.

The person we believe we need to be to be a success.

The person we believe we need to be to be a good parent.

The person we believe we need to be to be a good husband and wife etc., etc.

It seems this outer person is created over years and years of environmental feedback – much of which occurs in childhood. And most people don't even realise it's happened

### The Inner You

This is the person we all are inside.

The 'real' us.

The genius, problem solving, and creative being we were meant to be.

### The BIG Gap Between Them

For most people the disconnect between who people really are inside and who they project to the world is profound.

This gap is HUGE, MASSIVE and, in my opinion, the BIGGEST roadblock to achieving happiness, success and fulfilment.

And here's why.

There is simply NO WAY you can ever be truly happy if the day in, day out person you have to project to the world is NOT the person you are inside.

It's just too much work!

Trying to achieve anything meaningful or achieve any of your goals becomes infinitely harder (if not impossible) because you are never really striving for what the inner you wants.

You're trying to get something that you don't really want and probably in a way that doesn't really fit with who you are.

Now, perhaps this explains why some of the richest, most successful people on the planet are never really happy.

Could it explain why so many sudden fame and fortune finding celebrities are so fed up, end up abusing drugs and alcohol and spending months in the Priory eating nothing but shredded wheat?

I think it just may.

That's the bad news.

BUT – if you can truly align your inner and outer self then it's my belief that achieving what you really want becomes almost effortless.

I don't claim to be there yet. I still have my own 'demons' – we all do. I had a huge disconnect and I've still not fully closed the gap.

But what happens when we begin to align our inner and outer selves?

OUTER PERSON       INNER PERSON
*(what the world sees)*      *(the real you)*

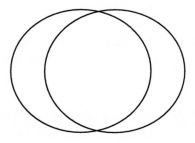

As we begin to align our inner and outer selves we move towards CONCENTRICITY; A place where our outer actions match with our inner self.

And when that happens it's like the floodgates have been opened. All of a sudden the roadblocks 'melt' away, the 'fears' of failure start to subside and like the afterburner on a jet plane we can accelerate towards our 'true' goals at a pace we never thought possible.

*"HA! That sounds great Henry. But I'm really not sure I can swallow that. Sounds like you could be talking a load of old cobblers?"*

Are you thinking something like that? I don't blame you if you are – I'd be thinking the same.

But what if it's true? And what if I can help you align your inner and outer self and help you accelerate towards your goals like never before.

Would that be worth 30 minutes – at most an hour of your time?

GOOD!

Because the exercise I'm going to walk you through changed my life and I didn't even realise it.

I looked back at my response to the exercise I'll give you in a moment after a number of years and was astonished. The notes I had written were so close to what my life had become it scared me. From how much I earned, to where I lived, what I did with my time, with who and even the clothes I wore.

I was half way to my ideal life and had got there without consciously even trying.

Try it yourself...

### Exercise One: Your Perfect Day

Simply WRITE DOWN (with a pen and paper – do not just think it, you must write it down) what your IDEAL, perfect day would be like.

Really...the best day you can possibly think of. From the moment you wake up to the moment you go to sleep.

What time do you wake up?

Where do you wake up?

With who?

What's the first thing you see?

What do you smell?

245

What kind of bed are you in?

What are the sheets made of?

And on and on. Absolutely every possible detail of your PERFECT day. And there are three rules to adhere to:

### Rule #1:

You MUST be happy to live this life every single day forever.

### Rule #2:

There are NO limits at all! <u>Absolutely no limits</u> to what you do on this day. DREAM as big as you wish.

### Rule #3:

Be VERY detailed. For example, don't just say you live in a big house. What is the house made of? How many rooms does it have, what colour is the roof, what is the drive like, what is the garden like?

Do this exercise on your own because for some people it exposes things in their life which even their closest companions would not wish to see...

Your description should read almost like a long diary entry.

And that's it. You need do no more than get VERY, very, very clear about what your perfect day is like.

Begin writing now.

## Exercise Two: How to Gain Unstoppable Influence on Your Market

I've been pretty lucky in being able to move into many different marketing environments and do very well.

And I've been able to do that by getting deeply 'in-tune' with those markets I work with. You see, people act largely based on emotions.

And people buy (in particular women – that's not me being sexist – don't tell me off - I didn't make the rules) based on emotion first and logic second. That's kind of accepted wisdom nowadays.

But the question I'm always asked is HOW do you develop the ability to influence people on an emotional level?

And the answer is in all sorts of ways – many of which I discuss in this book.

But my SECRET WEAPON – and something which can make every piece of marketing you do 'light years' more effective is in fact the 'Concentricity' exercise you just ran.

What I want you to do is run the same exercise but from your ideal client's shoes.

What would your average ideal client's perfect day look like – in depth?

Once you know that and you can feel like they feel then everything you do both in business and every piece of marketing you run will be naturally guided toward your ideal clients ideal day.

I mean – think about it for a moment.

If someone came to you and said they could help you get all the feelings you described in your 'perfect day' would you listen? Of course.

Now granted, not all your clients and prospects are the same and we may even 'turn a few off'. And no – I'm not asking you to start giving away £10million Sunseekers – but that's not the point.

The point is that once we know how we can truly influence the inner self of our prospects and clients – we can do what no other business in your category can...

We can begin to build a truly deep bond with our market.

So... now I ask you to run the same exercise as you ran for yourself but for your ideal client. But who is your ideal client?

- What is his/her name?
- How old are they?
- Are they married?
- Do they have children?
- What kind of work do they do?
- How do they dress?
- What kind of lifestyle do they lead?

- How much money do they have?
- What hobbies do they have?
- What are their biggest hopes?
- What are their biggest fears?

And then I want you to write about them in detail – like a story. I'll start off an example for you:

Debbie is 37 years old, she is a well-dressed, professional lady – in fact she is an accountant......

I won't continue the example because I don't want to influence what you write...

Grab your pen and paper now and write a story about what your ideal client is like...

So, now you've decided who your ideal client is we need to run the ideal day exercise you ran for yourself for them.

All I want you to do is write down (with a pen and paper) what your IDEAL client's perfect day would be like.

The same three rules as before apply:

Rule #1: They MUST be happy to live this life every single day forever.

Rule #2: There are NO limits at all! <u>Absolutely no limits</u> to what they do on this day. DREAM as big as you wish.

Rule #3: Be VERY detailed. For example, don't just say they live in a big house. What is the house made of? How many rooms does it have, what colour is the roof, what it the drive like, what is the garden like?

Your description should read almost like a long diary entry. Documenting every single part of their day - from what time they wake, with whom, what do they see, etc, etc, etc.

Be as detailed as possible. Begin writing now.

## And that brings us to the end of these rather strange exercises

I know they seem a little 'weird'. I make no apology for that.

These are some of my SECRET WEAPONS. Things I have rarely, if ever, revealed before. Don't be fooled into thinking they are 'silly' or 'beneath you' or 'pie in the sky'.

For a moment imagine what it would be like if every single action you take every day is effortlessly in tune with taking you ever closer to your ideal, perfect day. By knowing what it is – that begins to happen.

And now you also know what your ideal clients ideal day looks like.

That makes it a little easier to have them pay attention to you. All you need to do is fit the benefits of your product or service and your story into helping them achieve their ideal day – or AT LEAST give them a little touch of the paradise they're really after...

Enjoy...

# INDEX

# Double Your Money
# Back Guarantee

## "Implement the Ideas in this Book and If Your Business Doesn't Grow While You Sleep then We'll Double Your Money Back"

Dear Reader,

No fine print here just an honest guarantee.

If you honestly feel you've done your best to implement the ideas in this book and your business hasn't grown while you sleep then you're welcome to claim double your money back.

Simply copy this page, complete the form and fax it back to us as below – INCLUDING a copy of your original receipt.

NOTE: Only one guarantee per individual, household, family or organisation of any kind. Valid for one year from purchase.

-------------------------------------------------------------------

Name _____

Business Name _____

Address_____

Town/City/Postcode _____

Email _____ Telephone _____

Reason for claiming under guarantee_____

**FAX this form to +44 208 181 7632**

# FREE Offers and Resources from the Author Henry Baker

# Free Stuff Linked to this Book

To help you get full value from this book,
there is a collection of

# FREE BONUS GIFT RESOURCES

waiting for you at:

**www.GrowYourBusinessWhileYouSleep.com/freegifts**

- **FREE E-Mail Course**… extension of the book – enrol today!

- **FREE Tele-Seminar** with the Author

… and every other extra resource referred to throughout this book.

# Free Newsletter Offer

## *Special Free Gift from the Author*

Copy this page and fax to +44 208 181 7632 or go to
www.GrowYourBusinessWhileYouSleep.com/freegifts

# FREE
### Test Drive Two Month of Henry Baker's Gold Inner Circle Membership

1. Two months of the Sleeping Profits Newsletter
2. Two months exclusive audio or video CDs
3. Gold members restricted access materials.

There is a one-time charge of £10 to cover shipping and handling for both months of the FREE Gold Membership, and you have no obligation to continue at the lowest Gold Member Price of £37 per month (£42 outside UK). In fact, should you continue with your membership, you can later cancel at any time.

Name_____ Business Name _____

Address _____

Town/County/ Postcode _____

Email _____ Phone _____

Credit Card ☐Visa ☐Mastercard ☐Switch ☐Solo

Credit Card # _____ Exp date _____

CSV (last 3 digits on back) _____ Fax _____

Signature _____ Date _____

Providing this information constitutes your permission for
Henry Baker and his associated companies to contact you
regarding related information via above listed means.

### "Finally! Your Chance to *Grow Your Business While You Sleep* as Author Henry Baker and His Team Create and Manage Your Entire Online Marketing Program!"

Dear Reader,

For a limited time Henry Baker will be conducting one on one consultations with serious business owners who meet a strict application process.

Successful applicants will be given the chance to have Henry and his team build, implement and maintain everything you need to attract and keep the best clients on a 'Done for You Basis'.

To apply, please request an application form at:

**www.GrowYourBusinessWhileYouSleep.com/apply**

NOTE: Consultations and 'done for you' campaigns are offered on a first come first serve basis and Henry reserves the right to refuse applications without explanation.

# Notes

Lightning Source UK Ltd.
Milton Keynes UK
29 September 2010

160538UK00003B/18/P